THE LAW OF THE FIST

INTRODUCING
THE (MOH) - TEMPLE - SYSTEM

BY
H.H. The Dalai Seng Shi
Grand Master O.E. Simon

CANADA ♦ GOLDEN BELL ♦ MCMXCIX

1st Edition published 1969
2nd Edition published 1989
3rd Edition published 1995
4th Edition published 1999

Canadian Cataloguing in Publication Data:

Simon, O. E. (Olaf Emil), 1929-
    The Law of the Fist

4th ed.
ISBN 0-9683504-4-5

    1. Kung fu. I. Title

GV1114.7.S46 1999   796.815'9   C99-900617-7

Published by: Golden Bell Publishing House Inc.
            P.O. Box 2680
            Grand Forks, B.C. V0H 1H0

Printed in Canada
Artwork by J. Vensel

FOREWORD

It is my sincere wish to contribute to the history and culture of our countries. For this reason, I am dedicating this book to each and every individual reading it. In a time when the values in our society are challenged and the glorious history of our past is taken for granted, let us not forget how valuable the gift of peace is — a gift which must be cared for if its value is to remain. Throughout the past century, the United States and Canada have grown up together like two brothers. The common border is ample evidence of a peace-loving people. This border has become the longest unarmed boundary in the entire world, where man may walk free and exchange the precious contributions of his cultures without domination. Let us therefore benefit from the knowledge of the Orient, yet not forget nor cheapen our heritage, which has miraculously created a bond of friendship stronger than those of any other nations, a century of understanding, of love and of peace.

> - **His Holiness The Dalai Seng Shi**
> **Grand Master O.E. Simon**

His Holiness, The Dalai Seng Shi,
Grand Master O.E. Simon

History of the TEMPLE KUNG-FU Organzation

The word Kung-fu in itself tells very little of a system which originated in China. Most of all is the term Kung-fu not understood in China proper and instead referred to as Shaolin or Sil Lum athletics. The concept of 'Wu Shu' is known to entail the Sil Lum practices which are today placed in the category of the Martial Arts but in essence do not really belong there. Our modern grouping system decided to place this art into this classification for a better public accounting of the related activities inherent in this field. Kung-fu, a term the immigrant Chinese coined in North America, however, does some justice in describing a system which is uniquely different from anything else which circulates under the image of the collective Martial Art scene.

The Temple Kung-fu group has reverted back to the original concept of this art, which is understood as being Kung-fu, the foundation of all the existing Martial Arts combined, be it Judo, boxing, Aikido or any other known system practiced today. The word Kung-fu describes time and work in togetherness; hence, the word Kempo or Shaolin or Wu Shu (as it is sometimes referred to in China) are in essence all one and the same. The claim that Kempo (meaning simply - the law of the fist) and Sil Lum boxing are something new is clearly false. New Kung-fu groups quickly began to adapt to the demand of the marketplace giving themselves different, good sounding names, clinging to anything which would bring authenticity to their cause. In one case a follower walked away from his master and created a 'Honan Shaolin Wu Shu' group of students probing into the past, writing and visiting Red China (the land which now hampers the old Buddhist Chinese temple masters in their beliefs) posing with false monks in front of the ancient shrines at the threshold of the Shao Shi Mountain - "monks who are more interested in tourist dollars than in the art". Noted masters, less known to the general public, left China after the Boxer Rebellion and still more left China after the ensuing Civil War, living predominantly in North America unnoticed for their great skill, remaining loyal to the code of their temple. On occasion they decided to appear in public meetings, demonstrating their skill in order to aid in the traditional spiritual revival only to remove themselves again after being betrayed by students. A well established circle lived for a few years around Ark Yue Wong in San Francisco but fell into oblivion after his recent passing.

The "Venerable Master", Grand Master Simon met the latter about twenty-five years earlier, removing himself from the international scene after being elected to lead the Neo Ch'an Buddhist Temple. During childhood he was instructed in the concepts and methods of the temple arts as a student of Master Fu Yen. Having practiced and studied the Honan and Fukien Shaolin methods, he has blended the skills of both eras and integrated them into the Temple, meaning, that all recognition of achieved learning will again only come from the sacred halls of the Temple. Traditional values forbid any Buddhist priest to announce or advertize

any given titles or honors other than those which are pro-
nounced by the Temple, henceforth, is the background of
the now established "Dalai Seng Shih" only known to a
handful of masters who were instrumental in the re-creation
of the arts in North America.

His Holiness, the present Dalai Seng Shih, former Grand
Master Simon, now World Leader of the Temple, upholds the
23rd succession of the Tookien Shaolin Monastery together
with the 2nd most distinctive person of the Temple, the
most Gracious Reverend, Guardian of the Temple, the next
Dalai Seng Shih to be, D. June Simon, known by the Temple
name "Nanlao". (Previous 21st succession was held by
Grand Master Lin Fie Hung and the 22nd succession was
entrusted to Grand Master Li Kwin Yan.)

The Neo Ch'an Temple decided to retain the well-esta-
blished term reflected in the trade name of 'Temple Kung-fu'
for the Shaolin Temple Arts to permit better public iden-
tification of these skills, its methods being only taught in the
"Temple Kung-fu Studios" which are accredited by the
governing Buddhist Temple. These studios have no connection to likewise sounding establishments.

The work "The Law of the Fist" is not meant to serve any
individual for the purpose of total instruction but to give an
account of the general spiritual outline, a mere introduction
to some basic movements which are shared by all systems
and yet which are so necessary to train more advanced
motions in the style. The long arm style, the short arm
version, the Tie Chie Ch'an Kung and the Tiger are not discussed or shown nor are the Muscle Change Classics a part
of the discussion. Forms of meditation and means of spiritual alertness are being discussed in the book "Cosmo-
genesis", a modern concept of an age-old principle to uplift
the faltering, deprived and forgotten ones. This latter work
should be obtainable in any good book store.

This introduction was given by:

The Neo Ch'an Buddhist Temple of Canada
P.O. Box 2680, Grand Forks, British Columbia
Canada VOH IHO

*Should you require any further information about the
Temple please write to the above address.*

Grand Master of Style in Form —
D. J. Simon "Nanlao"

CONTENTS

THE LAW
OF THE FIST

THE MOH (TEMPLE) SYSTEM

INTRODUCTION

See here the empty valley.
No master's eye observes the student now.
Time has passed in centuries,
Taking with it the knowledge of the empty hand,
Preserved for the most dedicated ones.
The ones whose soul and heart withstand
And use with dignity such perfect skill.

But time has changed many things, and what was considered ample protection a thousand years ago is definitely inadequate for our modern society. This is true especially if one depends only on two empty hands, as did the traveling Buddhist monk when he refused to carry a weapon, believing that his God-given natural weapons were sufficient.

The empty hand, today publicized as Karate — then known as Shao-lin-ssu, Kung-fu, (Hua Ch'uan, "flowery hands") — was practiced by monks who, because of the respect they had for their religion, were ardent believers in nonviolence. To them, the highest achievement they could attain during their lifetime was to reach enlightenment through the training of the mind and body. Thus the Buddhist monk Bodhidharma (known to the Japanese as Daruma) has been credited with introducing the first scientific self-defense system into China. These techniques were later to be adopted by the island of Okinawa. Within this time, numerous changes in the system were made and many different motions were added. New ideas and carefully devised training methods resulted in new masters founding new styles, such as the

White Crane system, the Hung system, the Li system, and many others. It was during this time that the Moh system came into being.

As there was not a plentiful supply of masters, it was regarded as a privilege to be taught Kung-fu. Thus the student had to prove his intentions to be honest and his desire to be fervent before a master would consider him as one of his disciples. Some students had to travel five hundred to one thousand miles in order to seek a master of reputation. After the master was found, there was no guarantee that he would consider seeing or speaking with the student. Because the secret training methods of such techniques as the ch'i; the panther punch, and the butterfly kick were jealously guarded, the master was very cautious in selecting his students. For this reason, the master would often let a student wait days before recognizing his presence. If the student was considered for acceptance, he then became the object of many exhausting tests. Once these tests were successfully passed, the master would invite the prospective student to enter his living quarters and share a meal with him. Even here the only concern of the master was testing and observing the student. Many obstacles, such as supplying no eating tools, were placed in the student's path. The student's intelligence would be judged by the manner in which he handled these situations and his attitude by his show of respect and behavior towards the master.

The Moh system, as all other effective systems of that time, was extremely well guarded. Thus, up to this very day, its existence is not common knowledge. Despite the extensive publicity given to Tai-chi-ch'uan and other Kung-fu systems, the Moh system has retained a very high degree of secrecy. However, there is no mysticism connected with these techniques though many of the hard and soft movements appear mystical when one observes their execution in air. The system itself is thought to be named after the master who created it. The so-called "inner" and "outer" schools of Chinese boxing are both more or less a part of this system.

The Southern Chinese hand movements, the footwork of the Northern Chinese systems and a combination of several Kung-fu styles (for versatility) merged together to form the Moh system. The four sets which are taught demand endless repetition and accuracy if they are ever to become of value to the practitioner. Solid and heavy movements suddenly erupt into fast, explosive motions or slow, concentrated, horizontally and vertically flowing motions. The breathing method will change accordingly from holding the air, expelling it with violent pressure, or inhaling it in complete relaxation — always emphasizing the fact that the air must escape after the technique, not during its execution. The reader will understand this more thoroughly once he attempts the throwing and evading techniques, as explained in later sections. These techniques require different breathing methods for each defensive and offensive application. The slow and soft breathing method is extremely helpful in developing the ch'i — not to mention its unsurpassed value as a healthy exercise. The value of these exercises finds its explanation in the philosophy of the art of Kung-fu — breathing for peace, strength and kindness, meditation for the mastery of the mind (enlightenment), for wisdom, and for the understanding which encompasses the circle of life.

HISTORY

OF

KUNG-FU AND KARATE

* Practice Form   (see back lining)

I. Section I: *Shao-lin ssu*

When one realizes that Shaolin Kung-fu has been in existence for more than fifteen hundred years, one can understand the difficulty in gathering authentic historical facts pertaining to this art. Indeed, both the countries of origin, India and China, were continually in a state of political turmoil, due to their warlords and civil wars. This and the fact that they suffered constantly from natural catastrophes and diseases explains the lack of good historical records.

It is thought that the first primitive forms of *Kung-fu* were developed in India. Eventually, these forms gained entrance by means of religion into Chinese monasteries. Later, used by the monks for protection on their long journeys as they traveled from one monastery to another through wild and distant country, *Kung-fu* became an art worth knowing. It was especially convenient for them, due to the fact that it not only offered protection but was acceptable in their religion, the philosophy of which stressed nonviolence. Another, the monks need not rely on external weapons for defense. The training methods soon proved also to be of great physical benefit to their practitioners.

Since these methods of boxing involved an increasing number of very versatile techniques, as early as the Ch'in Dynasty (250-207 B.C.) many decisive self-defense systems, Chiao-ti for example, could be found. During the later Han Dynasty, this particular system was given the name of "Shou-pu." As time advanced, the once primitive versions of animal-copied fighting methods — as found in India — developed into accurate, systematically trained physical-combat forms. These new forms were again revised by a medical doctor and surgeon called Hua T'o (A.D. 190-279). He devised the first successful sequence of movements to relieve emotional tension, which, by liberating the mind, aided the practitioner in acquiring better reactions and control of techniques. It was his teaching that physical exercise executed with reason, and breathing combined with motion, secure good health and proper circulation of the blood. Supplying the body with more nourishment resulted in the rejuvenation of the body as a whole and longevity of life. Hua T'o has been credited with devising the bear and monkey movements and with the invention of new training methods. He is also believed to have found cures for damaged tissues and injuries incurred by the practitioners. However, it was not until Bodhidharma added to physical conditioning a form of mental training, which united certain movements with breathing and meditation, that true *Kung-fu* came into being. This school, known as Ch'an (Zen in Japanese), was the lifetime teaching of Bodhidharma. According to Bodhidharma's philosophy, the state of enlightenment could be achieved on earth by means of meditation.

While in India, Bodhidharma became a devoted disciple of the priest Prajnatara. Here he was made the 28th patriarch of the Buddhist faith after Sakyamuni. At this point, Bodhidharma began to acquire a much keener interest in the accurate teaching of Buddhism, as he himself was striving to attain Buddhahood. When he learned that Buddhism was being misinterpreted in China, as far as fundamental thinking was concerned, he decided to journey there and correct these errors in the Buddhist religion. Passing through the various kingdoms of China, Bodhidharma found Buddhism to be very formalistic, overburdened with pompous ceremonies and laden with symbols, all lacking in depth of thought. The Chinese architects created magnificent buildings and beautiful new monasteries, which, in carvings and sculptures, emphasized the achievement of Buddhahood after death rather than during the learning period on earth. Entering the kingdom of Liang, Bodhidharma heard that the Emperor Wu, of this kingdom, was teaching Buddhism in direct contradiction to the Buddhist doctrines. According to Wu's theories, enlightenment or Buddhahood could only be achieved after death. So it happened that Bodhidharma continued his journey until he came upon the Liang capital, Chin-lung. Here he met with the Emperor Wu. Bodhidharma must not have been able to influence Wu, for in the annals of history it is said that he left the kingdom very soon after this meeting. Also supporting this is the fact that the knowledge of the Ch'an schools was not pursued in the kingdom of Liang for some time after Bodhidharma's departure.

From Liang he traveled into the kingdom of Wei (Hunan Province), arriving at the ancient city of Lo-yang. Bodhidharma then continued south, finally entering the Shao-lin monastery.

Bodhidharma's school of meditation must have borne a close relationship to the Indian yoga, as the rituals and procedures are almost synonymous with those of the Indian meditative system. Historical sources claim that Bodhidharma, upon his arrival at Shao-lin-ssu, went into meditation for nine years gazing at a wall. Disciplining the body in such a way — through breathing and meditation — the mind could regulate the inner body and govern both emotion and behavior to the strictest degree of perfection. Upon emerging from his meditation, Bodhidharma surrounded himself with his disciples and discussed with them a sequence of already existing movements based on his own interpretations. The I-chin-ching and the Hsien-sui-ching books on the military arts were in his possession at the time. It was this added knowledge, in combination with the Ch'an meditation, which has created the authentic Shao-lin-ssu *system* — the original of almost all the presently practised Oriental fighting arts, the true beginning of modern Karate.

However, the primitive form of Chinese boxing, prior to its Ch'an influence, had spread from India several hundred years ago under an unknown name. As well as traveling

18

in a southwesterly direction, it is also possible that the migration of the Indian version of combat took place in an easterly and westerly direction. Evidence supporting this theory is found in the mention of a type of fighting called "pancratium," which existed in Greece prior to the founding of Bodhidharma's Shao-lin-ssu. Annals of history state that pancratium permitted the use of the feet, the hands, twisting of the limbs and strangling. Pancratium, because of its violent nature, was never permitted to become an Olympic sport. It soon became extinct. Traces of certain stylistic movements bearing a strong resemblance to those of Kung-fu have also been found in Portuguese Africa. These same techniques were carried across the ocean to South America, where they are now practised in Brazil under the name of "Kapueira."

Shao-lin-ssu, however, was still secretly practised, and over many centuries it slowly changed, finding its way north and east. Many more different styles were derived from the Shao-lin-ssu method, and new and better knowledge resulted in the practise of highly advanced training methods. These methods were jealously guarded in order to maintain the strictest possible secrecy. Tien-hsueh was believed to be one of these systems. It was thought to have specialized only in the touching of the nerve points. The secrets of this style have been adopted and blended into other systems; and thus many of the characteristic feats, such as the delayed touch of death, which requires decades of diligent training for effective application, have been lost.

II. Section II: *Decline of Ch'an School and Expansion of New Systems*

During the Ming and T'ang dynasties, Shao-lin-ssu reached its highest state of perfection. Test devices (see picture) and even a legendary pathway were created in order to establish and secure solid standards. Wooden dummies, lethal clubs, knives and swinging swords were located in both walls bordering the pathway — the purpose being to test the skill of the disciple when confronted by aggression taking any form. Hidden mechanized relays were activated as soon as the student stepped forward, each triggering the attacking robot catapults. It was not only the weight of the person applied on the floor but also the intensity in which he dealt with a released dummy that decided the number of attacks to occur next. Only a few men are known to have completed such a test without injury or death. A final obstacle, taking the form of a round, heavy cauldron, was placed at the end of the passage blocking the doorway to freedom. The walls narrowed to the point where they practically touched the cauldron, which was kept extremely hot. The student was required to lift or push the cauldron from its position, at the same time burning his body severely, in order to liberate himself. By lifting this device with the arms the impression of two half-moons was burned on each forearm — the mark of Shao-lin-ssu. This later was replaced with the symbol of the tiger and the dragon.

Kung-fu attained its highest level of development in Southern China during the T'ang and Sung dynasties. Through the influence of natural environment, climate and ways of living, the Southern *Kung-fu* styles began exhibiting dis-

20

VENSEL

tinctive characteristics which differed from the authentic Shao-lin-ssu system. Soon the North also changed and improved its form of *Kung-fu*. The result was the creation of two basic schools of *Kung-fu:* the Southern school and the Northern school. The Southern school emphasized very few foot techniques, rather concentrating on the versatility of the hands and the control and force of the mind. The Northern school preferred the multiple use of foot strikes trained in correlation with meditative force.

As the expansion towards the west continued into Manchu, the Northern styles and the Southern styles, through merging together, created the first eighteen standard hand movements on record. At the very same time as the Shao-lin-ssu *Kung-fu* reached its highest point of perfection, a new school of *Kung-fu* was founded in the vicinity of Mount Wu-tang. Its style was soon to be called Wu-tang-shan Kung-fu, or that of the "inside school," the name being in opposition to the Shao-lin-ssu "outside school," which, as we recall, originated in India. Although Wu-tang-shan was considered the fruit of an all-Chinese invention, it had little value as a combative system, for it failed to achieve and maintain the philosophy of Ch'an (Zen) through uniting the the mind and the body as one. After leaving the monasteries, often called "the homes of meditation," and being introduced to large societies, the Shao-lin-ssu method, over the years, also lost its connections with meditation. The Chinese hand-to-hand combat methods began to concentrate more and more on the Kang-fa and Jou-fu systems, which, incidentally, exhibited a definite relationship to the tai-chi-ch'uan system. Jou-fu, compiled principally of grappling and throwing methods, became the source from which most of the defensive techniques against attacks originated. Although almost all the schools guarded their training secrets, the common society was trained due to the family system, wherein the culture of the past is handed down to the present generation in order to preserve its existence for the future. The valuable influence of meditation, as taught and practised by the monks, finally became publicly extinct in its connection with the military arts. Yet the expansion of the knowledge of certain systems continued merely by existing on the reputation developed over the last generations. The many wars of the past during the T'ang, Sung, Ming, Han and Ch'ing dynasties also aided in both promoting and destroying the combative arts of this era. The promotion can be found in the training of larger masses of societies in shorter periods of time. The destruction lies in the resulting devaluation of the precise and distinct systematic approach involved in individual training, thus ending the direct relationship between the master and his disciple. Respect, patience and desire were no longer necessary requirements as they had been in the past under the very demanding Shao-lin-ssu masters.

Now that larger areas were becoming involved, new problems began to arise. Factors such as distance, language and natural obstacles tended to interrupt and delay rapid progress. One could imagine the obvious opposition caused by the Pacific Ocean to the east or the great desert to the west. The fact that Kung-fu was exported from India to China across the wild terrain of the Himalayan Mountains is indeed a phenomena. However, a very valid explanation can be found if one considers the dedication and the depth of the connection between the Buddhist monasteries. Thus, what may seem a phenomenon to us was to these people a very natural, dutiful pilgramage.

Authentic reports prove that the introduction of Kung-fu into Korea preceded the introduction of Kung-fu into Okinawa by several centuries. The Korean Kung-fu was a form of military discipline known as "farando," which involved the use of the feet, elbows, fists and head in its techniques. By combining farando with some native Korean techniques, the warriors of Silla produced a method of fighting known as "taiken," by which they defeated both Koguryo and Paekche. Silla renounced her identity and the new nation of Korea was formed. These people now adopted the same attitude towards the martial arts as the people of Silla possessed. Thus, during the Koryo period (AD 918-1392) the prior eighteen hand techniques doubled to become the thirty-six trained-hand movements known as "chabi."

However, political and social unrest soon resulted in a complete turnabout, and the once successful martial arts now entered into a period of decline which was soon to become permanent. After the revolt against the Yi dynasty (AD 1312-1910) the arts were placed under strict control. Finally, during the Japanese occupation which followed, they were outlawed. However, the Japanese warriors quickly absorbed whatever knowledge these Korean arts had to offer before outlawing them. It is even believed that the Korean wrestling, today known as Sumo, was introduced to Japan at this time.

But it was not the introduction of the Korean martial arts which lead to the serious practice of Karate; rather, it was the passing on of combative *Kung-fu* from China and Taiwon to the Ryukyu Islands (Okinawa) which seemed to exert the greatest impact.

III. Section III: *Modern Karate*

Upon observation of the history of man in general, it has been established that the desire for freedom and the right to choose one's place in life has made man fight to maintain those things which are of value to him, especially when deprived and exploited by such people as warlords. The Island of Okinawa, over a long period of time, has been subject to occupation by the Chinese and to conquests by the Japanese. Its shores were raided by the Wo-k'ous (Chinese pirates), and when under foreign domination the natives of Okinawa rebelled against being used as slaves and servants, they were brutally dealt with by the occupation authorities. The mounting resistance of the Okinawans resulted in the confiscation of their weapons and more unreasonable punishment by their invaders. Rather than encourage subjection amongst the people, this treatment created in them a strong urge to liberate their island and a serious desire to perfect the weaponless hand-to-hand combat. Soon the short sword, or "sai," replaced the common battle sword. It could easily be hidden and its multiple purposes as a versatile fighting instrument became more important, especially when Kung-fu methods of blocking and attacking were practised and trained in conjunction with it. The short sword, or "sai," had a definite influence on the creation of the Okinawa-te form of Chinese Kung-fu. During more peaceful periods some Okinawan masters had the desire to learn Kung-fu more accurately and also to study more than one Kung-fu system. Several Japanese masters, such as Master Sakugava (from the city of Shuri), Masters Shorei, Itosou, Higaonna, Kobayashi and

Uechi left their island to study in China. The legend reports that Master Uechi went to China to study the art so that he would be capable of seeking revenge. But as a result of his long and serious study in China, he learned to conquer not only his body but his mind as well. He returned home to Okinawa a young master, humble and peaceful, seeking fulfillment in teaching. His system is still being taught today.

Some of these masters created their own methods: they bettered and simplified various Kung-fu systems; and they used a systematic method in searching for degrees of effectiveness. In their individual styles — which, I might add, were trained to the height of perfection — they became almost impregnable. The strong influence of the Chinese Hung style and the Tong Long Pai (mantis system) can be traced in some Okinawan styles. But the Ts'ai (or Choy), showing fast foot-stepping techniques as well as weaving and shifting body movements, has never influenced the strong, stable, patient fighting method of any Okinawan system. The one flaw evident in these new Okinawan teaching methods was, however, the loss again of meditation. Renowned styles such as Goju (hard-soft) ryu (style), devised by Chojun Miyagi, a disciple of Master Higaonna (Shito-ryu), came into being. Prior to the accurate individual systems of the later periods there were three basic Okinawan styles practised, each named after a city or province of Okinawa. Shuri-te ("te" meaning hand), Naha-te, and Tomari-te were the systems which influenced the all-Okinawan style known as Okinawa-te. Since 1480, as the influence of Chinese Kung-fu (not the Shao-lin system) began to circulate throughout Okinawa, practice sessions seem to have become very strict and brutal, especially after the occupation in A.D. 1609 of Lord Shimazu (Japanese), which is known to have lead to the most serious and dedicated practice of Okinawan Karate ever to exist. Since then many styles were taught, some of them merging into other Okinawan systems, until in 1929, the Karate genius Gichin Funakoshi introduced Okinawa-te to Japan as true Karate.

Gichin Funakoshi may be considered to be the father of modern-day Karate, for he emphasized to the youth of his country the great importance this combative form had in its physical and mental values. Karate-do, or "the way" of Karate, as a sport, self-defense system and military art has been publicized through his never exhausting demonstrations and lectures. In his early years it was said that many of his fellow Okinawans were hostile to his idea of teaching this sole Okinawan art to the general public. The Japanese universities, however, recognized Funakoshi's objective and sponsored his classes. Soon many universities engaged in the art of self-defense as a competitive sport, maintaining and preserving the skill of their masters. But only after the end of World War II did Karate begin to attract as much, if not more, publicity as Judo. Fascinating demonstrations of throwing, punching, kicking, all done with unbelievable speed and power, made Karate the most devastating self-defense system ever practised. Unfortunately, the impression was aroused that Karate was an extremely dangerous art involving lethal attacks with one's hands alone, which were, of course, heavily calloused and deformed; also, that the sole aim of the Karate practitioner was the destruction of bricks and boards in order to demonstrate his "superhuman" strength. Because Karate has been commercialized beyond reason (for example, one can frequently obtain package deals such as one free trial month of lessons or other promises), a once honorable art now lay face down in the sand, a victim of the "civilization disease." The intention of Master Funakoshi to maintain the honor of Karate and to preserve it as an art, as it was once practised, has found little ear in either the Occident or Japan. Many people are attempting to introduce Karate as a Japanese invention by stressing foreign terminology, in the belief that this will increase the authenticity of their theory. However, no art or instrument once mastered remains the art or instrument of a country or district; rather, it becomes a part of the individual mastering it.

Thus, Karate is not Oriental or Occidental — it is what it

is, a method of attaining high physical and mental skill for one's own betterment, health and confidence. Used as a competitive sport, it is certainly one of the most modern and exciting contact sports. As well as being enjoyable, Karate also manages to connect many countries and people together, its main objectives being to unite, to understand, to learn and to better all things. Therefore, if we give credit to anyone then let us pay homage to history, whose records speak of the former pioneers of modern Karate as being the Chinese.

THE

THE MOH (TEMPLE) SYSTEM

THE PARALLEL TO NATURE

SPRING—represents Youth—development

SUMMER—represents Ripe Age—work and result

AUTUMN—represents Old Age—results with the addition of experience, betterment

WINTER—represents the Age of Wisdom—perfection of mind and body, peace, and enlightenment.

AUTUMN

WINTER

I. *Its Philosophy:*

Slow as the snow is melting to water
Is the spring turning towards the winter.
Midnight and light may change in between.
Over the circle of planets watches one master,
Never retiring in order to seek all beginning.

How many millions of years have gone by since the day of creation? Life has maintained its circle of being, birth as the beginning and death as the ending, yet still remains. Whether or not the end means a very new beginning or the beginning is a continuation of the ending, no earthly being knows. The overall magic circle of life remains, the change-over from one form of existence to another, from light to darkness and from summer to winter. Man has learned to value the presence of light; he has learned to welcome the first signs of the arriving spring, to celebrate in gratefulness and to worship life. His religions are evidence of his gratitude to Nature's universal greatness. As there is rain and snow, warmth and cold, darkness and light surrounding us, we are involved in seeing and feeling, in applying our senses to what is happening. As man learned to worship, he also learned to protect, to defend, to preserve; and by doing so, to love and to hate. How much room, how many thousands of years or myriads of universal cycles are lying between love and hate? Or how small really is the distance between these two feelings if love was associated with reason and hate was connected with understanding? To protect, to preserve, to defend and to uphold man's achievements by these deeds we may recognize the value of man in general, be it a nation or an individual. The training of the mind, educating it and disciplining it in unison with the body, will give us the means by which we may participate as beings — human beings. In ancient China it was the Buddhist monks, their teachings and their striving for enlightenment, which led to the effective unification of mind and body, to the mastering of violence through hard training and the invention of their own forms of defense for the protection of their religion and their principles.

But the spreading of this art to unworthy people soon found its result in the decline of Kung-fu. Having been put to misuse, Kung-fu lost its character. It took the reasoning of the young Kung-fu disciple Moh to reinstate the values of the religious monks. In his mind lay the desire to give his art more than just the physical benefits of speed and force. Practising so that his feeble body became stronger, he lost much of the prevailing urge for revenge which had remained in his heart, due to the poor treatment he had received when he was a small, frightened young boy. Evidence of a growing confidence, through his fervent studying, now displayed itself. Realizing this change in himself, he observed that his practising held a much greater hidden value. For now he had attained good health, alertness and a new, ardent desire to seek perfection in his training. All through his life he learned and practised, finding the circle of life through the art which he studied by repetition.

Now, perhaps, one sees that the Moh system exists not without reason, for it follows Nature, passing through the four characteristic periods of life:

Period

(1) youth — associated with desire (defense) late stop

(2) ripe age — (offense) immediate stop

(3) old age — a combination of both

(4) age of wisdom — exploring, preserving, betterment, peace

If there is truth in everything one can see in Nature, from the rising of the sun to the reflection of a mountain peak in the emerald waters of a peaceful lake, or the thunderous trembling of a gigantic wave thrown by the forces of motion upon the rocky shores; if there is truth in what can be seen, then it stands to reason that there must be equal truth in those things which cannot be seen. After exploring such thoughts and comparing them to the trained visible force, the result of a kick or a blow, it is evident that in meditation the hidden force or the inner strength (ch'i, or Japanese Ki) could have as much effectiveness as the visible impact of a movement.

How violent seems to be the eruption of a volcano, forces liberated which were once dormant, to the eye not visible — undoubtedly another form of Nature's own inner strength! Meditation creates the inner force in us; if the mind and body have direct, equal influence on what one is doing then the proper reaction towards danger is secured, provided that equal training results in accurate physical application. Meditative forces then must be trained in accordance with the type of defense or counter used. To be capable of recognizing in time to counter or defend requires good reflexes, which undoubtedly is the subject of meditative training — seeking peace of mind and permitting the mind to have a true state of observation lying in peaceful readiness. Then, not being influenced or preoccupied by outside thoughts, even a false movement will be recognized, and simultaneous attacks can be dealt with as efficiently as possible. Peace of mind, through training and the desire to achieve perfection while practising, and learning and the continuance of learning long after acquiring a thorough background of knowledge, will be the result of a well-interpreted philosophy of the Moh system.

II. *Its Application:*

In all sciences Nature has been man's greatest teacher,

from Daedalus and Ikarus to Montgolfier, from Newton to Freud or Konfutse talking to Einstein. Though the differences between their application and their theoretical explanations of the sciences may seem gigantic — coming from both the ancient sagas and the authentic annals of history — we have learned from these men, who dedicated themselves to the protection of man and the betterment of the world in which he lives, the laws of nature. Forces of destruction are also a part of Nature, a part existing within himself, which man has never actually learned to control. Being involved in the art of Kung-fu, one is introduced to many stages and phases which one has to learn to accept. Dealing with force involves great preparation and willingness, on the part of the student, to accept a certain degree of punishment while studying. In the past much has been written about the physical application of Karate (Kung-fu), and many authors have succeeded, more than ever before, in bringing the art closer to the public. However, we still suffer from sensationalism — the deadly art of mayhem and what have you not. Admitting this in general opens the door for the most important question of all: If death is the true and final result of applied Kung-fu, then why may we not benefit, through the true aim of the philosophy, and attain peace by hard practice, using the force within us to create a new energy directed towards the maintenance of peace rather than violence?

III. *The Class:*

At first, we learn how to stand, how to behave, then how to move and how to defend and to counter. Peace is silence. The Kung-fu student is calm as well. His desire is directed towards obeying and studying. He enters the training hall — white walls washed clean, furniture for necessity only, far removed of comfort and luxury, yet interesting to the eye, for these humble surroundings are filled with a demanding spirit: they hold the truth of mankind.

In order to pay his respect to the master of the past and

to his present teacher, the student will bow upon entering and leaving the training area and before the start and finish of his practise. This is true regardless of whether he is by himself or accompanied by other students. As we admire the achievements of all these combative systems of the Orient, we therefore believe in the basic upholding of their traditions. However, we do not worship; subsequently, there is no reason to bow until the head touches the floor. A very slight nodding motion shows that the student has understood and that he now, after having indicated his respect, is willing to discipline himself, unconscious of all external influence, concentrating only on his efforts to attain skill.

Learning requires time. Time requires patience. Patience teaches one to progress wisely.

STANCES

I. Introduction to All Stances

One of the most important movements in life is the phenomenon of walking. To quote Darwin, it took man hundreds of thousands of years to finally walk on two feet, raising himself to a position wherein he could attain perfect balance. The skeleton of man, unique in its construction, is a tower of strength held together by joints, tendons and muscles. The body can stand rigidly, jump, run or even fall if trained well enough.

A stance is a position in which man is erect and stationary. Motion in the normal (forward) direction helps us to retain balance easier. Forward motion eliminates small disturbances coming from all directions threatening our balance. But when one stands erect, having both feet close together, a more acute sense of balance is required. In such a position it would be extremely easy to disturb any person's balance. In order not to fall, one would have to go into motion and step in the direction in which the balance was being broken. But if one would know how to stand properly, with strength and good balance, one would be capable of coping with a larger amount of force directed against one's balance. In a situation in which we are required to contend with an external force (an attack), it is essential to be well versed on the maintenance of balance while in different positions, as well as to actually retain balance at this time. Even more so, it is important to know how to handle the opponent's balance; one must apply the right technique at the right moment with the minimum of effort.

According to the ancient Chinese standard of teaching, a disciple had to prove his desire to learn by very lengthy standing. Often a year passed before the master taught anything other than how to stand and step, using various stances. (Many modern schools can no longer afford to adhere to these old standards, as the commercial approach has created an erroneous relationship between student and teacher. Suddenly, the teacher becomes a salesman and the student a customer which indeed is not only a disgrace to the tradition of the art but also establishes disrespect for the title of "master.")

A strong stance will allow for the inclusion of many more position aspects in the vast knowledge of *Kung-fu*. Having mentioned the importance of the balance factor in basic martial arts, one need use little imagination to realize how the loss of balance can often bring about an easy defeat. Being forced off balance will result in the loss of the hands and feet, which are necessary for defending oneself by blocking, punching, pulling and kicking. Rather, the hands are occupied in protecting the body from injury incurred by the fall, and the feet are helpless without the support of a stance. In short, a broken physical balance creates also a broken psychological balance. Therefore, all students should seriously practice the positions of the different stances. One has to be accurate and patient and learn the meaning of each and every stance. Only then can one appreciate the following training, as one has experienced the changeover from one position to the next, combining stepping and punching, blocking, throwing, jumping and kicking, as well as avoiding and falling, in order to defeat one's opponent.

In conclusion, the accurate stance and the knowledge of the different variations of the stance are the keys to an effective defense. Again and again, the student must repeat. As he learns the fundamental structure of the Kung-fu stances, he must also become self-critical, analyze his errors and correct them.

By observing and comparing the very basic approaches of Kung-fu instruction with the techniques taught in Karate, a layman would be incapable of determining whether Karate or Kung-fu was being taught. However, the concept upon which *Kung-fu* is based is the establishment of a strong body frame capable of delivering force as well as receiving punishment, yet flexible enough to apply throws, to fall and to avoid through a simple twist of the body. The maxim that if a *Kung-fu* man is brought off balance he is defeated holds no truth. On the contrary, a well-advanced student will be taught how to fall, to throw and to deliver fatal blows and kicks after being brought off balance and, more especially, how to fight on the ground.

All this is so very detailed and specialized that it is possible in this book only briefly to touch on the vast field of *Temple System* basics. All other material will be later introduced in a complete final work on the advanced Moh system. The aim of this art is to provide protection for the weak, including the handicapped, as long as the student is willing to sacrifice and devote himself to many years of serious studying and to specialize in the particular field which, because of its movements, suits his physique. The amount of knowledge one has accumulated is not necessarily as important as how well this knowledge has been learned and to what degree it has been perfected. One fact remains for the novice — a strong stance means security; a weak stance results in the instability of both mind and body.

II. Explanation of Each Stance

Front Bow Stance

The front bow stance — or forward stance, as it is often called — is one of the most common basic positions used when facing an opponent. (Figs. 1, 2) The stance is deep and opens at an angle of approximately 45° from the centre of gravity; the toes of the front foot are slightly pointed to the inside; and the knee is pressed strongly to the outside, thus creating tension in the leading foot. This will protect

Fig. 1　Fig. 2

the knee joint from injury in case of an attack from the side, and aids in the stability of the stance. It is very important to observe the correct position of the back foot. For the effective delivery of force, the knee should remain locked in order to eliminate any severe rebound from the force applied. A bent knee assumes the role of a shock-absorbing spring, accepting a large return of force rather than concentrating as much power as possible on the point of impact. The toes of both feet are gripping the surface, which further increases the stability of this stance. In observing the photographs, one should pay the greatest attention to the posture of the body as a whole: the right hip is solid and placed in a forward direction; the lower spine area is turned well inside; the shoulders are down and pushed back; the chest well formed to the front; and the head kept straight. The body weight is equally distributed over both feet. While executing a kick or a punch, the student should not raise the supporting foot (heel), but rather have the same firmly planted on the ground, thus giving his technique stability and good balance. (Exactly the same procedure is followed in the execution of the right forward stance.) This stance is called the bow stance because of the similarity between the two positions; for, in archery, when the bow is drawn, it also results in an extreme amount of force being controlled under tension in basically the same position.

46

Broken Bow Stance

This stance is a prime example of the characteristically coiled Kung-fu position. It waits in readiness to release its potential energy, and is capable of an immediate change of position if necessary to attack or avoid an offensive move by leaping toward or away from the assailant. As shown in Figures 3 and 4, the left broken bow stance can be assumed with little difficulty if one at first positions oneself in the left front bow stance, then pulls the back foot until the toes of the right foot have reached the level of the heel of the left front foot. Both feet are approximately twelve to

fifteen inches apart and almost parallel to one another. Observe the right hip. You will see that it is slightly arched to the right and that the supporting knee of the right leg is lowered and well bent. The weight is distributed in an approximate ratio of 7:3, or 70 per cent to 30 per cent, the larger portion of the body being carried by the right leg. The left hip is drawn backwards.

Riding Horse Stance

As the name indicates, this stance bears a strong resemblance to the position a person would adopt while riding. Of course, there is some difference between sitting on a horse and standing in the same position without being held up by the horse's body. In the latter case the legs have to carry the full weight. Supported by the arched legs and a well-formed spine and chest, this unique position (Fig. 5)

Fig. 5

forms the foundation from which great strength may be emitted. All histories of the Karate and Kung-fu systems breathe of this position. As far back as 1,400 years ago, one could find the monks of the Shao-lin monastery meditating in the exact same stance. The fact, therefore, that the ancient masters had quite a reputation for their lengthy holding of the "horse" is understandable. Advanced students were required to stand sixty minutes or more in order to test their strength and to force the body and the mind to fight against the increasing pain and signs of exhaustion. Great accuracy was stressed as far as keeping the legs strongly arched outwards with the knees pointed to the outside. Even today many Japanese systems are extremely specific in teaching this stance to their students.

In order to attain the highest degree of proficiency, this stance has to be kept low (Fig. 6). A low horse position permits the application of strength to the fullest, be it striking or throwing power. (However, advanced skill is

6

Fig. 7

required in order to be capable of kicking effectively from this stance.) Upon observing and comparing the illustrated horse stance (Fig. 7) with a common front bow position, one can quickly perceive that from a position having a low-centred gravity, such as the horse stance possesses, it is definitely easier to throw a larger and far heavier opponent than oneself. Much dispute exists amongst Karate men as to how far the feet should be apart in a strong horse position. Because of the vast differences in the physical structure of individual bodies, some people have extremely long legs but a very short torso, or vice versa. Thus, the proportions of the body do not, at all times, permit an ideal execution of the horse stance. In order to give an accurate measurement for each individual, the distance between the supporting legs can best be determined if one kneels on the right knee (Fig. 8) in such a fashion that the heel of the left foot is in line with the right knee, then places two fists between the left heel and the right leg and turns slowly to the right. The result is a fairly accurate measurement of distance for the required separation. (Fig. 9) After a certain period of time, the student will learn to adapt his stance without the help of this kneeling position. (Fig. 10).

Fig. 8

Fig. 9

Fig. 10

(a) Moving from the horse stance

With adequate training one should be able, from this position, to move quickly in any desired direction. (Fig. 11) In order to provide more lucid understanding of the directed inside leg movements, this stance is photographed from the back. The left foot begins to cut diagonally at approximately 45° to the right, and is then forced into the horse position

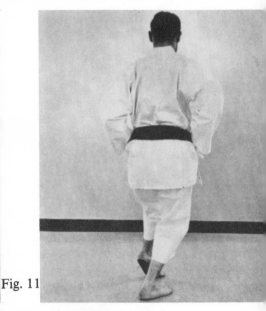

Fig. 11

to the left. The diagram (Fig. 12) indicates that the right foot remains stationary, pivoting only as the left leg moves into the new horse stance. Alternately, moving forward one raises the right leg in the very same way, assuming the new position and creating a pattern as shown in Fig. 13.

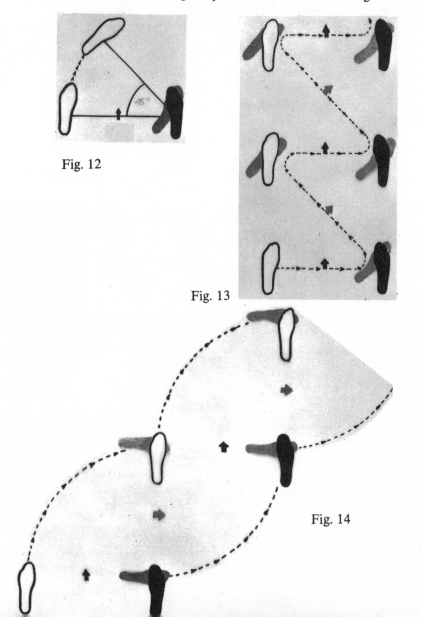

Fig. 12

Fig. 13

Fig. 14

Another method by which this stance may be used in defensive and offensive techniques is the box pattern. (Fig. 14) One proceeds in the very same way as before. As the left leg moves to the inside the entire body now pivots 90° to the right. Then the left leg is forced from the centre back to the left to form a horse stance position. (Figs. 15, 16) In explanation of the diagram shown, one behaves in the same way as before; however, instead of moving only 45°, one now steps a full 90° forward. Of course, it is only logical that if one wants to maneuver backwards the same procedure is followed as in the execution of a forward step, with the exception that the whole approach is reversed.

Fig. 15 Fig. 16

(b) Closing the horse stance

Prior to its change of direction, or before going into motion, the left leg returns to the centre of the horse position. Thus, the practitioner, while closing his stance, retains the utmost security, for the very vulnerable groin area is now protected against low attacks. Depending on the opponent's location, in view of one's horse position, or the number of opponents one has to cope with simultaneously, a different way of stepping may be justifiable. Remaining with the box pattern method (Fig. 17), it will, on some occasions, prove effective simply to swing the leg outside blocking the path of the aggressor's kick. (Fig. 18) Here the left leg is raised, the knee well bent; then, using body motion, it is turned to the right. The leg is held at 3/4 of the distance of the proper horse position while turning, thus making contact

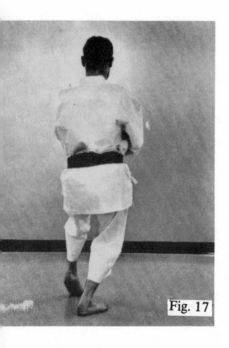

Fig. 17

Fig. 18

Fig. 19

Fig. 20

with the kick at half the distance. (Fig. 19) If the balance of the aggressor is broken then this technique has been applied accurately. (Fig. 20)

Yet another very important method of bringing the horse position into motion is the 180° turn executed to both the left and right sides. The two basic approaches are simple to remember, as the stepping is done to the left and right sides only. One leg remains stationary, the other crosses over the front or the back to the left or right, forming a complete 180° turn, depending on what position is required. To explain this best, note the basic position shown in Figures 21, 22 and 23. First step across the horse position, with the left foot in front, to the extreme right while turning the body. A new horse position, as shown in the photographs (Fig. 23), is now assumed. A change of 180° has been completed from the position held in picture 21 to the position held in picture 23; and a new horse stance facing in the opposite direction results. The same turn may be executed using a different

Fig. 21   Fig. 22   Fig. 23

Fig. 25   Fig. 26

method of stepping. In this case, one crosses behind the
supporting foot. (Figs. 24, 25, 26) The procedure following
is now precisely the same as that for the 180° front crossing
turn. Stepping in this fashion, an attack may be avoided
by simply shifting the body in a different direction. One may
also adopt a very new and extremely versatile stance, known
as the "X" or "twist stance." This position is often in-
cluded in the stepping direction for the 180° turn. (Fig. 27)
It will, however, be dealt with in a later chapter.

Fig. 27

57

Fig. 28   Fig. 29

Broken Horse Stance (Sumo Stance)

This position is also referred to as the "L stance." The basic posture has been copied from the horse stance, the one exception being the feet, which are pointing to the outside at an angle of 45° from the original horse stance. (Note Figs. 28 and 29) With such a position, one can easily defend oneself effectively from two sides and also possess additional lifting force. Figures 30a and b describe the exact foot position. The imaginary straight lines are extended through the heels, and should form a 90° angle at the crossing point if the positions of both feet are correct. Being posted like this, one can deliver foot strikes to almost all directions and use foot blocks equally as well. Note the sequence of pictures. (Figs. 31 to 36)

By observing these photographs one soon begins to sense the extreme versatility of certain positions. Of course, many of these motions can be executed from the common horse stance equally as well.

Fig. 30

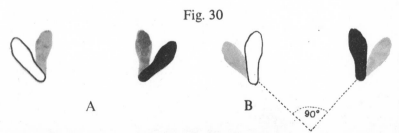

A   B   90°

Fig. 31

Fig. 32

Fig. 33

Fig. 34

Fig. 35

Fig. 36

Diagonal Horse Stance

The diagonal horse stance (Fig. 37) is usually assumed after the execution of a flying front kick. The descending body finds solid support for its weight in this unique spread-leg position as the bent knees absorb the shock from the landing impact. There are two basic versions of this stance: the left version, called the "left diagonal horse stance," in which the left foot is leading, and the right version, known as the "right diagonal horse stance," in which the right foot is leading.

Fig. 37

High Back Stance

One of the most difficult positions to execute is the high back stance. Though it is described as a high positioned back stance (Fig. 38), the body is in fact kept extremely low, most of the weight of which rests on the supporting back leg in a ratio of 60 per cent to 40 per cent. As the diagram (Fig. 39) indicates, the front leg is completely extended forward at a 90° angle to the heel of the right foot.

Fig. 38

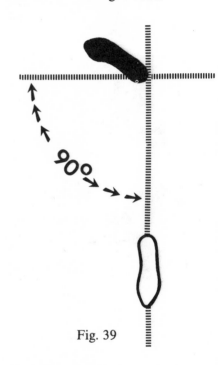

Fig. 39

The knee of the supporting right leg points slightly backwards at a height of approximately twenty inches from the floor. In throwing an opponent, one's attention should be directed to the supporting back leg. In the execution of a throw from this low position, a wrongly formed back leg would result in the injury of the knee joint. (Figs. 40, 41a-d)

Fig. 40

Fig. 41a

Fig. 41b

Fig. 41c

62

Fig. 41d

Upon observing the pictures pertaining to this back stance, one should note that the knee of the left front foot is kept slightly bent. The purpose of this is to prevent the joint from locking, as would be the case if it were attacked from the front. Again one must pay attention to keeping the body erect, with a well-formed spine. In all Kung-fu stances the solid torso will help to secure stability and handle effectively any force or balance problem; this is true especially if one attempts to throw one's opponent. The art of throwing, however, is so highly specialized and has so many important phases involving detailed knowledge that it requires a much more explicit, accurate explanation. Therefore, I shall leave the topic to a later chapter. When executing a throw from the high back stance position, one must first know how to block the arm and foot attacks of one's opponent. During the actual throwing, the defending person must collapse his stance while proceeding in the same line of motion as the aggressor and yet not lose balance. The right thigh will take the impact of the falling body after the knee of the same foot gradually bends until the thigh is only inches away from the ground. (Fig. 42) The correct execution of this technique requires much skill.

Fig. 42

Low Back Stance

Having first observed this stance, one is immediately aware of the strong relationship between it and the high back stance. Both the leg position and the entire body posture remain unaltered. However, one difference is apparent, the height is less. This new low position requires good balance and extremely strong leg muscles in order to permit the execution of precise blocking and countering techniques.

Leg-stretching exercises (Fig. 43) aid in the development

Fig. 43

of these muscles and joints so that they may carry the weight of the body and permit the student to move effortlessly in such a stance. At first glance, the picture of a man moving on the ground in this fashion seems absurd. The thought of maintaining balance alone is enough to dissuade anyone. But with diligent training, the results will prove very satisfying and beneficial. The supporting back leg is low enough to touch the heel. The heel is raised and the body weight is supported merely by the ball of the foot. (below) The

Fig. 43a

weight distribution is approximately 60 per cent to 40 per cent, the back leg bearing most of the body. Being only inches away from the floor, the front leg is kept straight, the knee joint locked. Note the contradiction to the high back stance wherein the emphasis is placed on avoiding such

Fig. 44

a position. (Fig. 44) However, when the foot of the out-stretched leg is placed at a right angle to the back foot, the knee joint will follow, to some extent, in the direction of the foot. Thus, an opponent, by stepping on this leg, would not damage the joint. A very small turning motion of the left hip (Fig. 45) towards the centre of one's own body will place the joint in a bendable position so that, if attacked, it may collapse, touching the floor. (Figs. 46, 47) An opponent underestimating this particular low position, can be stopped very quickly and thoroughly (Fig. 48) with powerful kicks and throws. Again, only detailed knowledge and serious practice will permit the efficient use of counter movements from this stance. This low position provides a base from which many extremely effective ground-fighting techniques may be applied.

For the benefit of the more intent student, this will be thoroughly outlined in a later edition.

Fig. 45

Fig. 46

Fig. 47

Fig. 48

67

Cat Stance

Upon first viewing this stance, one is instantly attracted to it by the strange likeness it bears to that of a cat about to lunge at its prey. Though the extended front leg appears harmless, one is acutely aware of its readiness to be put into full motion during the very next second. (Fig. 49)

The right hip is lowered and both feet are almost parallel to one another, the exception being the back leg, the foot of which is turned slightly to the outside. Characteristic of this stance is the raised heel of the front leg. Any body weight, being supported on the front leg is carried by the ball of the foot in a 70 to 30 per cent ratio. (Fig. 50) The upper body posture in all these stances should be constantly corrected so that: the spine is kept erect; the lower portion bent inwards; the chest well formed; and the shoulders held down and backwards. (Fig. 51) When done properly, the cat stance, with its extreme flexibility, allows one to maneuver easily and quickly.

Fig. 49

Fig. 50

Fig. 51

Fig. 52

Cross Cat Stance

A new aspect of Temple Kung-fu is the cross cat stance. Withdrawing the left foot, as outlined in our photographs (above) , to such an offset angle permits the easy application of a foot block. (Fig. 52). Not only blocking and stepping techniques are hidden in this stance but an entire arsenal of motions.

These must be dealt with more explicitly and will therefore be left for explanation in a later and more advanced book.

Side Cat Stance

For the execution of special foot maneuvers, the left foot is kept directly beside the right supporting leg, which is itself bent. (Fig. 53) Again the left foot is touching the surface with the ball of the foot only. From this position (here the left side cat stance) the left leg is capable of executing effective blocks against low kicks, especially stiff, low swinging kicks to the groin area. (Fig. 54)

53   Fig. 54

Twist or X Stance

By assuming a left front bow position, then cross stepping with the right foot (Fig. 55), one arrives at the twist or X

Fig. 55

Fig. 56

position. As the picture (Fig. 56) indicates, 70 per cent of the weight is carried by the front right foot, the left leg being slightly bent at the knee joint, the heel raised off the ground.

This stance is often underestimated as far as its versatility is concerned, despite the fact that it allows for at least a dozen effective kicking possibilities. To elaborate here, while explaining the basics of the Moh system, would only be confusing for the beginner. The picture sequence (Fig. 57) shows some of the possible techniques which could be applied from this stance.

Fig. 57

Narrow Kneel Stance

This position is quite easy to learn. Assuming a horse stance (Fig. 58), one turns to the right, bending the left knee deeply but not enough to touch the ground. Using accurate arm movements, it is possible to stop two opponents simultaneously. (Fig. 59) While the entire upper body is turned (here to the right) the feet as well point in the direction of the turn (right side). The narrow kneel position may be used just as effectively to the left as it is to the right.

Fig. 58

Fig. 59

Wide Kneel Stance

The wide kneel position is easily assumed from a front bow position. The knee of the supporting leg is deeply bent and only six inches off the surface. Figure 60 shows a right wide kneel position, with the left foot leading.

Fig. 60

Crane Stance

At the very beginning of this book, we explained that many Shaolin-ssu motions developed from observed animal fighting methods. For a human being to adopt the position of a crane, standing on one foot and having the other foot lifted off the ground, requires more than strongly developed leg muscles. One must possess a keen sense of balance in order to maintain this position for some time.

When assuming the right crane stance (Fig. 61), the opponent's attack is expected to come from the side. Standing in this fashion enables one to strike or block to almost all directions. (Fig. 62) The crane position requires concrete knowledge of the art in order for it to be used effectively. To remain flexible, for the purpose of fighting, one must bend the supporting leg (Fig. 63), in contradiction to the animal which retains a straight line in its stance. In the Moh System the crane position is not used as a base from which solid fighting is executed but rather as an intermediate position adopted during the changeover from one state of fighting to the next.

Fig. 61

Fig. 62

Fig. 63

77

Closed Crane Stance

In general, this stance is identical to the open crane position. Only the knee of the raised leg is kept straight, thus closing the opening to the vulnerable groin area. (Fig. 64)

Fig. 64

BASIC
STEPPING AND TURNING
TECHNIQUES

Fig. 65

I. Introduction

In the explanation of the common basic stances of the Moh system, some of the stepping techniques have been shown. In order for this system to be of value to the beginner, it is essential to show a variety of these movements, which are simple yet effective. On facing an opponent, as shown in Figure 65, the defending person standing in an upright position with both feet close together is well advised to step backwards, into a front bow stance, avoiding a straight line of fighting. Moving in this fashion will definitely benefit the defending person, for he will be going with the force of his opponent's attack, thus helping to avoid its full impact. In addition, he also is moving his entire body sideways, away from the forward direction of the attack, allowing himself room to defend with foot strikes as well as arm blocks, yet remaining outside of the main line of attack.

II. Techniques Explained

Slide Stepping

One of the most common stepping techniques, used in a situation where distance does not permit the delivery of a kick or a blow to the opponent, is slide stepping. (Fig. 66) The stance is brought forward by moving the back leg ahead to the front foot, then moving the left leg forward to form a new left front bow stance. Now the right leg is ready to strike.

Fig. 66

Cross Stepping

This method is equally as fast and strong as slide stepping; in fact, it is even more versatile. Cross stepping allows the full motion and turning range of the hips for half-circular kicks and side-thrust kicks. The picture (Fig. 67) explains how to cross step from a left front bow position. A side thrust kick delivered from this crossing position (Fig. 68)

Fig. 67

Fig. 68

83

can be done prior to the completion of a new position (Fig. 69) by using a kick instead of a step. The left foot is used for the foot strike. Almost the same cross-stepping method is used from a horse stance, crossing in front of, or behind, the supporting leg. (These techniques have already been explained during the introduction of the horse position.) (Fig. 26)

Fig. 69

Slide Leap

The slide leap form of advancing towards an opponent deserves special attention. Unfortunately it is rarely used despite its effectiveness in countering an opponent's attack. Just to show the explosiveness of the slide leap technique (Fig. 70), the actual time difference between these two opponents shown in the photographs would be only a fraction of a second. The reason for this is that the whole stance is brought forward in one motion. In true combat some Kung-fu men prefer to slide leap several times, during which they combine their defensive and offensive motions accordingly. Slide leaping can be done from almost all stances to all directions.

Fig. 70

85

Step Turning

As the X, or twist, stance has already been described, we know how to cross step. Therefore, if the student turns around 180° on this twist stance (Fig. 71) he will come to face the opposite direction in a front bow stance (one may also change from a front bow stance into a twist stance).

Fig. 71

Another method of turning used is the one shown in Figure 72, here executed from the left front bow stance. The right back leg is brought to the left foot. The body is turned on the spot, assuming now a right front bow stance. (The same method may be used accordingly from the right front bow stance.)

Fig. 72

THE
NATURAL KUNG-FU
WEAPONS

He who desires peace should prepare for war
— Vegetius.

In this book a simple, but explicit description has been given of the basic Kung-fu stances. As the natural weapons are a part of our body, they are dependent largely on its posture and position. Poor posture can influence the breathing capacity of the lungs and result in an insufficient supply of oxygen, which quickly causes a weak stance or faulty balance. In order to use these weapons effectively, they must be properly supported so that the application of the techniques is both accurate and secure. Upon realizing the almost infinite number of available techniques which can be executed with one's arms and hands, one understands why it would require at least two lifetimes to master all of the known movements.

Being man's most versatile limbs, the arms (which includes the hands) possess a wealth of motions. They can be trained for speed and strength, and are capable of changing direction instantly, pushing, pulling, grabbing, hitting, turning, lifting, punching, pressing and rotating. The possibilities of combined movements are unmatched in comparison to the other limbs of our body. As the legs and feet are supporting the body, and thus constantly engaged in the act of moving, it is obvious that they also possess great strength. However, their movement is more confined. The purpose of the legs (which includes the feet) is to bring the body into motion, to maintain its balance and, in the case of danger, to jump, run, step and slide towards or away from the attacker. Leg movements permit striking, blocking, swinging, hooking, bending, and kneeling. Yet without the flexibility of the body (the hips, the elasticity of the spine), our movements would remain limited. The spine supports the body and is responsible for the behavior of the limbs during a kick, stepping, etc. A throwing technique is dependent on the spine from the beginning of its execution until its completion.

One of the less obvious natural weapons, which is often neglected, is the head. Being supported only by the spine, tendons and muscles, it gives shelter to the brain, the centre of all our nerves, which direct and control the senses and forces of our body. Nature has protected the brain with a thick layer of bones in the shape of well rounded, self-supporting plates. However, a brutal blow to the head would easily disturb the functioning of the brain and, depending on the inflicted area and force of impact, could result in fatal injury. The many arm blocks available offer sufficient protection as well as leave enough room for the head itself to be used as a weapon. The neck muscles, which direct the movements of the head, have great strength and are capable of strong forward and backward motion. Thus a head strike against the bridge of the opponent's nose is easy to do and extremely effective.

If we were to summarize the natural weapons, their meaning and relationship for defense and counterattacks, we would define their range according to the three basic areas in which they may be applied. (See Illustration, pg. 156) The centre of the body offers many targets (sensitive areas), such as the stomach, liver, spleen, heart, lungs in the front and the kidneys and spine in the back. Arm and foot defenses cross the centre area for additional protection. Thus, a low arm block or a high foot block will protect both the lower abdomen and the chest.

The pictures and drawings will acquaint the reader with the natural weapons while in motion. The close-up photographs of the striking position indicate both the striking surface and the correct application. (pp. 93-102)

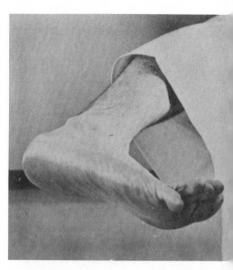

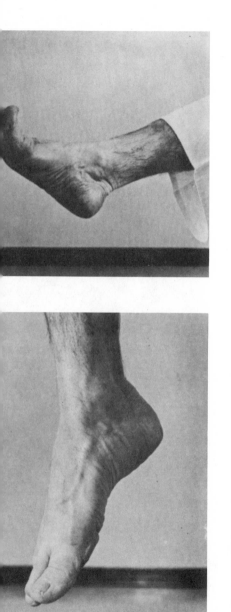

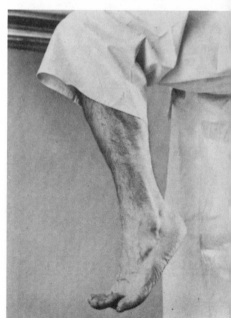

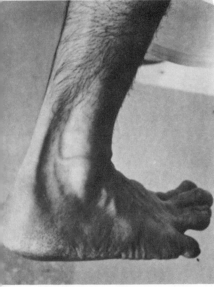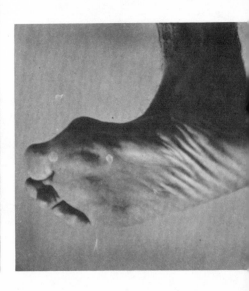

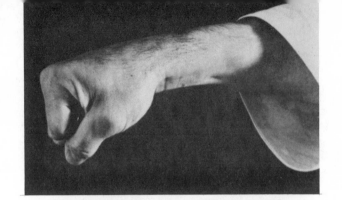

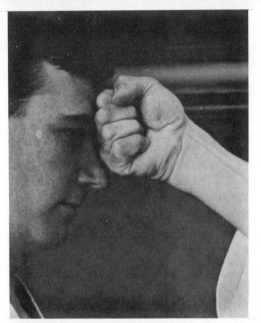

96

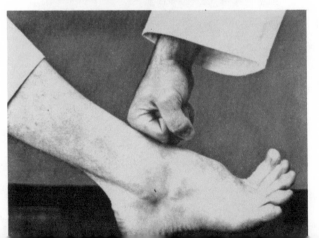

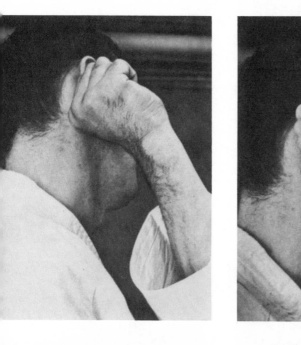

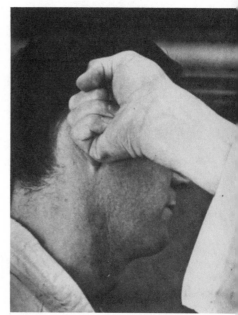

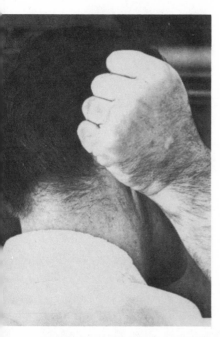

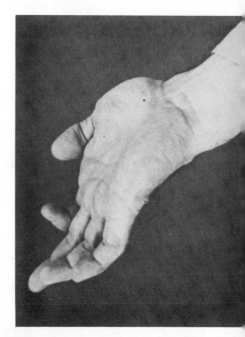

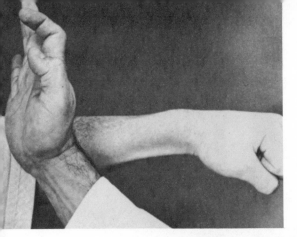

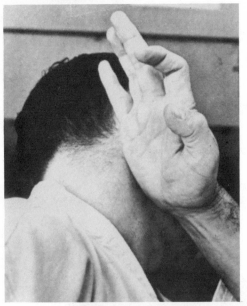

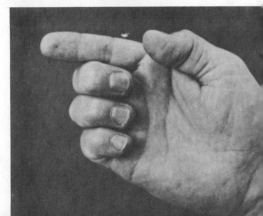

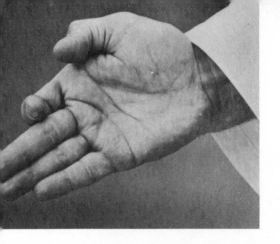

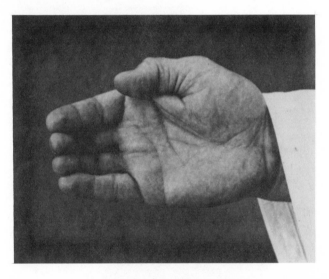

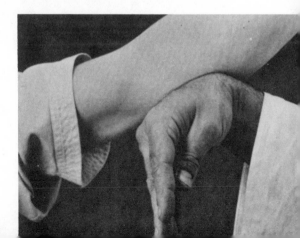

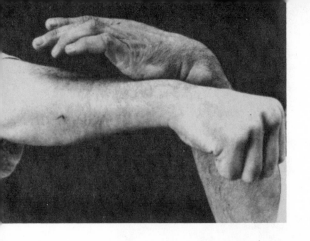

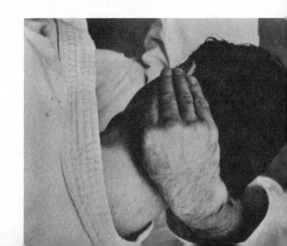

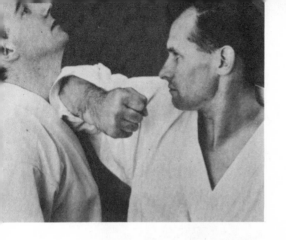

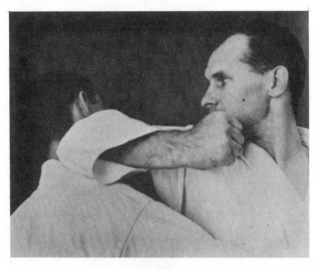

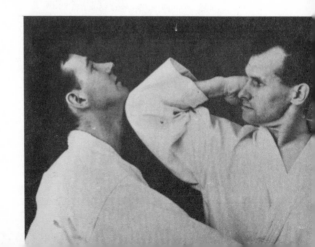

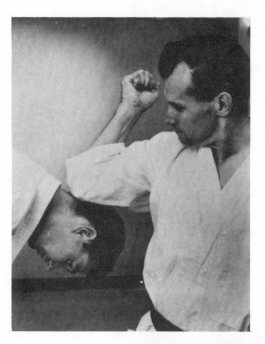

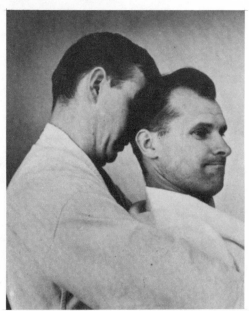

METHODS OF
TRAINING AND CONDITIONING

VENSEL

Just as the various Kung-fu and Karate systems differ in their techniques and philosophies, so do they differ in their training methods. If the belief that these systems hold great secrets bears any truth then here is where we must begin our search. To know exactly when to relax and when to resist, how to turn the fist while punching and how to pull properly without wasting too much of one's energy, these are the "secrets."

In general, the systems agree upon the very basic methods of training—how to step or turn, stand, fall and strike. A good system provides enough techniques to suit almost any physique; a poor system is one wherein the instructor has to force the technique on the physique of a person regardless of whether or not the practitioner benefits from it. Not every student is able to execute a high powerful side kick from the crane position or develop a strong circular back kick from a forward stance. In such cases, there should be an equal variety of techniques available to suit any physique, including the handicapped, thus providing all students with equally forceful and effective movements. Previous to this chapter, we have observed how the feet, hands, elbows and knees can be used. Of course, a slow kick will most likely not be as powerful as an extremely fast foot strike. Therefore, of first priority is learning how to strike, how to direct the natural weapon most effectively, how to focus a blow or strike without permitting a large return force due to the wrong application of one's own delivered strength.

Up to this very day, much dissension remains between Karate experts over the belief that it is wrong to raise the heel of the supporting foot during a front kick. Many of our Chinese friends still argue that a swinging high front kick can be done effectively only if one raises the heel of the supporting foot — which is true. However, these exceptions are usually recognized by other teachers once they are shown and discussed. For instance, in this particular kick the leg is kept stiff while striking, which is not taught in most other styles; therefore, a kick such as this requires special execution, but that does not mean that all kicks have to be done by lifting the supporting heel. After some discussion, it was agreed that most advanced kicks are to be executed using the same rules as new students adhere to — and that is not to lift the heel while striking. The Moh system uses a variety of stiff-leg striking techniques which are done in addition to all the known foot attacks. However, these foot maneuvers are only of value to a person who has mastered the very basics of Kung-fu, and they are therefore withheld in this issue of the introduction of the Moh system.

A very widespread form of conditioning is the striking of the hands and feet against hard surfaces in order to create calluses to reinforce the natural bone structure on the contact points of the limbs. The Moh system does not overemphasize such practices, though it does realize the importance of solid punches and foot strikes. The senseless exposure of the limbs to punishment, such as some systems encourage, often leads to the crippling of the joints and paralysis of an entire arm or leg. To study and train with reason, to approach intelligently such practices of conditioning, was the essence of the teachings of the ancient Chinese. Methodical, systematic instruction requires patience and a true desire on the part of the student. In contradiction to most of the existing schools, the Temple System will never guarantee a black belt or its equivalent in Kung-fu to any person, for it has as its sole aim the teaching and promoting of the philosophy involving the four phases of life (Fig. G). The sports version of combative Karate is a most welcome development for those who strive not only for explosive contact force (in which all systems are well trained) but also for the perfection of techniques and the attainment of skill. Even the least educated person is hesitant to accept the belief that brute strength alone is the key factor in victory or defeat. "What good does it do if one owns the force to kill with one blow five times?" argued a famous Chinese master after he had killed a tiger. The astonished crowd could not find any trace, whatsoever, of a blow on the animal — evidence of the inner, or invisible, strength for which this master had trained a lifetime. His hands were small, bearing no calluses, yet the killing of the tiger had proven that he owned far greater strength than most masters before him.

There are many stories which report such events in which great strength and far greater skill were praised. Undoubtedly, it is possible that a tiger's neck can be broken after dodging his attack and no visible mark or sign of struggle remain apparent. However, it would be wrong to conclude that this feat was accomplished using a fully grown animal. As strange as some of these reports are, and whether or not they are true according to our method of judging, there are great forces dormant in every human being; and it is only a matter of training to make them available and to learn how to apply them effectively. Though the earnest student practices diligently, it takes more than a teacher to cultivate the inner strength, for every individual responds differently to what has been shown to him by his master. However, once this strength is acquired, there is no need for exhibitions in which a man murders animals in order to prove his strength. To take the life of any living thing in order to prove to oneself one's own strength and skill is a form of madness and the work of one who seeks acclaim at any cost. True force is given to man only in the case of self-defense. These artificial attacks by animals, generally provoked or arranged, provide a sad example of the perversion of the mind, regardless of whether or not an excuse is found. Man's intelligence provides excuses for the benefit of his own conscience; thus, a very sound reason is found for all his deeds.

The frantic race continues. Now skill is exhibited by breaking bottles with the hand. The reasons — attracting public interest for the sake of publicity. However, it goes further, for publicity turns into money, and money, in modern terms, means ultimate and unquestionable success. Daring to propose that this idiotic sequence bears a relationship to the ideas of character building, peace of mind, confidence and health is in itself preposterous, yet it is obvious that these promoters hope to mislead the public with such "garbage."

Though it may appear that I have strayed slightly off the topic, I too feel it is important for people to realize the relationship between conditioning and the mind. To educate one's mind well and to learn to refuse to participate in such ventures as the killing of animals for the sake of personal gain is an initial step.

Physical exercise, done with reason, will gradually build up the body, loosen the muscles and strengthen them. In general, any kind of warm-up training is helpful — running on the spot, lifting of the knees to chest height, swinging of legs to the front, back, sides (Fig. 73), etc. One of the

Fig. 73

most important groups of exercises are the stretching exercises (Fig. 74), which aid in the execution of fast and powerful foot strikes. According to the age of the student and his past involvement in sports, the serious preparation for further study of Temple Kung-fu requires complete knowledge and proper application of these exercises.

Fig. 74

Knowing that it is essential to have a firm and solid stance in order to deliver force, we have chosen a horse stance as the training position for the basic punching exercise. Both fists are placed above the hip, as shown in Figure 75, palms facing upwards. During the forward motion, the

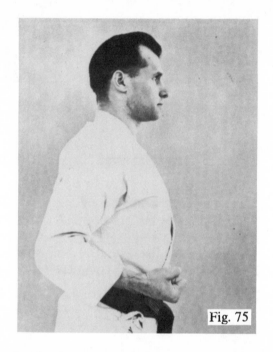

Fig. 75

right fist is slowly turned until it reaches the position of Figure 76, with the palm now facing down. Striking with the left fist, the right arm is pulled back with great force in the same fashion as it was brought forward. The left arm is simultaneously brought forward to its target. This exercise should be done slowly for many thousands of times, excluding, at the beginning, force and speed. As soon as one arm is fully extended, the withdrawing arm should be at the point where its movements first began, the side of the hip. As more speed and force are gradually added to these

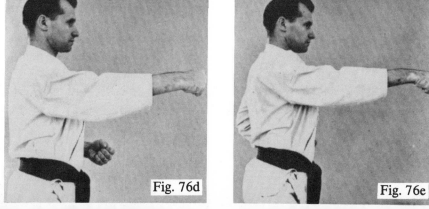

Fig. 76

Fig. 76a

Fig. 76b

Fig. 76c

Fig. 76d

Fig. 76e

punches, one must observe that the striking arm coincides perfectly with the withdrawing arm in order to achieve a more effective thrust. The shoulders must never be raised or slouched forward during the practice. They must be held strongly and erect, yet remain relaxed. The proper position of the shoulders enables one to maintain good balance and control throughout the delivery of the punch. (Fig. 77)

Fig. 77

One should never begin punching training with a striking board, as most students will at once concentrate on the striking object and neglect to withdraw the arm after striking. Once a habit such as this is formed an opponent is left with the opportunity of grabbing the arm or breaking the elbow joint with little effort. (Fig. 78)

Fig. 78

Fig. 78

The rising, or high, punch is of course done in the very same fashion as the middle forward thrust. It is advisable however, not to turn the fist as far as was shown before, but rather to turn the arm only half of the distance. The result is the delivery of a vertical punch, which, due to keeping the wrist straight, permits a stronger punching technique. (Fig. 79)

Fig. 79

After several months, the student has sufficient skill to strike at a hard bag (gravel) and, finally, on a striking post (which should be padded and flexible in order not to cause any joint damage). While training how to punch and to harden the fist, the student should learn to combine stepping and punching and kicking and punching, using all possible variations — leading with the left leg, punching with the right arm, punching with the left arm as he steps forward or retreats with the left leg, etc. But one's force depends very much on one's breathing techniques. Though one may have breathed slowly during the first punching exercise, this type of breathing will not always aid in the execution of a decisive, powerful technique. Accurate breathing, maintained according to the surrounding conditions and circumstances, will always unite the body and the mind. Here again, each different style carries with it different opinions. The Moh system does not apply the loud Ki-ai (a yell which involves the tensing of the abdomen and the body in preparation for the delivery of force). In order to execute this yell, one must open the mouth. According to the beliefs of the Moh system, this action will interrupt the flow of strength. A balloon, for example, when completely inflated, is supported by the internal pressure of the air. Thus, any external pressure, to a certain point, finds equal resistance. However, if the air is allowed to escape, the pressure within the balloon will be less and the surface of the balloon will therefore offer less resistance to any outside force. Thus, one can see that by permitting the air to escape through the mouth a great deal of resistance from within is lost. In the Moh system the air is held until the technique (punch, kick, etc.) makes contact; only after this time is it allowed to escape.

The purpose of using a yell during an attack is to disturb the emotional balance of the opponent, thus delaying his actions long enough to counter his attack and to inflict injury upon his body. In Temple Kung-fu this sound is not used in unison as is the Ki-ai; rather, the yell is done prior to the attack so that the mouth is closed again, allowing no air to escape during the actual delivery of force on the target. When performing more than one technique in a very short time, this breathing method will prove extremely helpful, for the complete sequence of movements will be executed continuously as one attack, without interrupting the flow of motion through inhaling which would weaken and endanger the successful application of these Kung-fu techniques. In any case, it would be wrong to inhale deeply while located in the immediate striking area of an opponent, for the body is as well engaged in the vital functions of life. Its reflexes, to a certain extent, are occupied in trying to secure an adequate supply of air directed by the subconscious and conscious mind. A well-trained aggressor would recognize this type of situation immediately and naturally take full advantage of a poor breathing habit such as this.

Many different methods can be utilized in the training of rhythmic breathing to nourish the blood and tense up the central muscles for protection and strength. The following method is easy to copy and has great value in aiding in the development of force and endurance.

The first step is to assume a horse position (Fig. 80), having both arms ready to begin punching. The fists are slowly opened while both the arms are simultaneously raised, turning the wrists in such a way as to have the index finger pointing towards the back of the horse stance. During this

Fig. 80

Fig. 80

motion, one begins to inhale slowly and softly through the nose (not the mouth) until the arms have reached their highest point above the head. Now pull the arms downwards past the chest. At this instant, the right fist closes: the left open hand is placed on top of it. The inhaling now ends and the exhaling procedure begins. The escaping air is forced slowly but strongly through the throat. As the left open hand presses downward and away from the chest, one should begin to resist, with the right arm, against the downward pressing hand. Tension arises because of the two contradicting forces, and the pressure which is executed on the lower abdomen, as a result, will build a strong midsection and increase the blood circulation. However, one should approach this breathing method carefully. Using too much tension during this practice can cause an oxygen shortage in the brain, which at first appears in the form of drowsiness. One should observe these signs of warning and at once discontinue any further repetition of this exercise. As it is the aim of all Kung-fu training to achieve good health, one must of course train hard and seriously; but this does not mean that one should overtrain and foolishly destroy weeks of work through careless practice. Symptoms of distress and slight balance disturbances are an indication that the body does not function properly and any further strain will definitely cause injury. Though in the Moh System we follow a hard pattern for conditioning the mind and the body, we do not promote an unreasonable training cycle but rather slow, systematic training to assure that all body portions are conditioned equally well for better force and true skill.

In ancient China, true Kung-fu was practiced only for defensive reasons, and the conditioning at that time was somewhat different from today. Foot strikes, for example, had to penetrate the armor of an opponent and a blow of the fist had to have sufficient shock to inflict injury through a helmet. To deliver a kick against a wooden shield or throw a punch at a metal helmet required not only strength but the knowledge of how to train the natural weapons to reduce injury while exposing them to hard surfaces such as those just mentioned. In the first Shao-lin monastery, the emphasis was on individual training in adherence to the religious belief which recognized only the natural weapons for the use in self-defense. However, the persecution of the Shao-lin monks by desperate warlords led to the opposition of these stringent rules; and when the second Shao-lin monastery was built, they began training political refugees, whom they had given asylum in their monastery, in offensive combat. The aim, undoubtedly, was revenge and the overthrow of the warlords.

As many other worthwhile inventions of man have been put to misuse, so the Shao-lin boxing method was misused upon its introduction to the soldiers. Generals and emperors learned to appreciate Kung-fu skill, and soon many of the warlords sought out instructors for their troops. Some masters, because they were forced to teach against their will, taught only the physical aspect of Kung-fu, preferring to take the wealth of their knowledge with them into their graves. Soon many more people were able to perform Kung-fu motions, but not for the benefit of the art, as they knew nothing about breathing or meditation. One Chinese report tells of a master who purposely taught his style wrongly while in captivity. Because he never revealed his deception before his early death, these disciples practiced his system for quite some time before realizing that they had been misled. His moral responsibility forbade this master to train the enemy in his skill. In this way, he retained his loyalty and honor.

Aside from the conditioning of the striking surfaces of one's natural weapons, it is essential for the student to attain first the skill to defend himself. Force is only as good as the person knowing how to deliver it. Even then there is no guarantee of victory if one's opponent is well trained and knows how to handle brute strength. Anyone can learn how to break boards and bricks by simply hitting hard enough and neglecting the health of the body. Those who wish to acquire this skill need not seek out a Kung-fu studio, for such a person is only interested in showmanship and not in the art. No matter how hard the striking side of a hand may develop, never will a fist have more force of impact than a simple hammer. What does breaking ten bricks prove if one cannot defend oneself against a weapon?

Knowledge and force are essential. Neither one can exist without the other. If a choice is required then skill would of course be of first priority. A knife and a hammer become worthless weapons against a skillful Kung-fu student. If it were a case of life and death, skill and experience are guarantees of victory rather than strength and blind courage. Psychology has established the fact that strength causes false confidence, and brutality combined with such strength are the characteristics of a street fighter. One should never underestimate any opponent, no matter how many years one has been trained in the combative arts. Man is, after all, only human, and thus not above making errors, such as losing his footing by stepping in a hole or slipping on ice or gravel. Good balance and the ability to devise a counter-attack, though at a disadvantage oneself, can only be the result of skill. If we have mentioned the importance of breathing as a necessary training method, the ability to maintain good balance is equally important. Because the purpose of this book is the introduction of the basics of the Moh System, breathing has been briefly mentioned only, for it is one of the most involved techniques used in controlling of force and physical and mental balance, and thus is subject to serious scrutiny at a later time.

The kidneys and lungs are responsible for the body's balance of acids and so are quite influential over the healthy development of any human being. Many of the secret techniques operate in this field. Our body is dependent on its ability to see, breathe and maintain balance. The Moh system basically directs its vital techniques to these three major areas. Having successfully disturbed one of these body functions, the attack of the remaining two becomes much easier and the final defeat occurs much more quickly.

When talking about balance, we include both physical balance and mental (psychological) balance. It is common knowledge that the sense by which one maintains one's physical balance is directed through the organs of the inner ear known as the semicircular canals. A sense of balance is created through little fluid-filled structures in these canals. Millions of small fibres of hair wave in this liquid, reacting upon the motion of the head and the force of gravity. Once signalled of a change of direction, the brain activates the muscle sense to maintain balance accordingly. The sense of balance is so very delicate that any slight interference, no matter how minute, activates a muscular reaction directed towards the maintenance of balance. However, if a violent assault occurs in the form of a pushing or pulling motion the balance of the common person is easily broken. Thus, all the various stances have been devised for the purpose of securing balance, or so that a changeover from a position involving a disturbed balance to a new stance can be inacted. Non-resistance — a very special field in the Moh system — plays a vital role in regaining or mastering one's balance. The art of falling, in order to seek a new position while taking the opponent into the fall, is also one of the more involved techniques of the Moh system. Both of these shall be left for the advanced student.

The ancient Chinese had a very ingenious method for training balance. This was an arrangement of many different tree stumps, all one-half to one yard apart, each varying slightly in height, on which the student learned to walk. At a later time, jumps, leaps and complete prearranged sets were executed on these stumps in order to show the master the degree of perfection of balance and the skill attained. Occasionally — to avoid brutal fights and to discourage young teachers from challenging their own masters — the same arrangement of tree stumps was infested with very sharp-pointed bamboo rods. These were placed in such a fashion that if a contestant lost his balance and missed one of the stumps he would fall on the lethal rods, proving his confidence to be false — as such, accepting the severe punishment for challenging his master.

Our senses perform a vital function in all combative arts and thus deserve a good deal of attention. If one has developed these senses by training and repetition one will be able to preserve them. Even upon reaching an advanced age, one can cultivate these senses through daily practice. The advanced Moh system introduces sets of exercises which specialize in the sense of touch and the reactions resulting from various forms of contact. This training will call upon the body as a whole, cultivating dormant senses and instincts which man has lost through the influence of civilization. Of course, there are no miracles, nor is there a set pattern by which one may react accurately on the basis of one's instincts. The training and refining of one's instincts is an art in itself and requires years and years of patient training.

If one is confronted with an opponent the knowledge of balance and balance reaction is essential for an effective defense. (below) The reason for assuming many stances while

BALANCE AND BALANCE REACTION

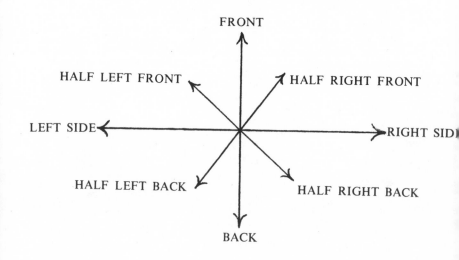

learning is to ensure that the balance of the student is constantly tested and improved. As a stance is at first taught while remaining stationary, the addition of movement requires good balance on the part of the student and the ability to retain an accurate posture while executing techniques. Leaning forward during a punch or a kick can be disastrous, especially if one's opponent is experienced in the combative arts. A toreador could never fight a bull without his skill and knowledge concerning the behavior of the animal. Side-stepping is one of the first actions against a forceful assault. When the thrust of power misses the intended target, physical and mental disorder of the balance senses results. Once the opponent is placed in this type of situation, one strong kick or blow often will decide the outcome of the fight. (Fig. 81) Another common procedure would be to break the opponent's balance after avoiding his

Fig. 81

attack by pulling, pushing, throwing, tripping, etc. (Fig. 82)
Attacking the supporting leg is also a very effective and
brutal method of breaking the balance of an assailant. (Fig.
83) Various foot strikes and blocks are aimed at breaking

Fig. 82

Fig. 82

Fig. 83

125

the knee joint of the supporting legs while stationary or being in motion. (Fig. 84)

Fig. 84

If it is possible to influence the opponent's mind in order to delay his actions or his intentions we may say that we have now disturbed his mental balance. This can be done in many different ways. One of the simplest techniques to produce this situation is the piercing yell which stuns the opponent, permitting one's own successful attack, or delays the assailant's action long enough to protect oneself. Again one should observe the proper breathing method and close the mouth after the "yell" has been executed. Through meditation one can train the mind to disregard any external attempt to influence the actions of the body. Meditation is extremely difficult to explain on the written page and cannot be learned without the presence of a qualified instructor. The most common mistake while learning to meditate is to occupy one's mind through concentration. The beginning and the end of a practice period are the most suitable times in which to prepare the student for meditation. He is asked to be seated in the "half-lotus" position (Fig. 85) and to place his left hand loosely on the palm of his right hand. (Fig. 86) Of course, one has to observe the correct posture. The eyes should rest approximately two yards away on the floor in front of the student. They must not concentrate on anything in particular. Such a resting position, if repeated often enough, will permit the instructor at a later time to introduce serious meditation for the benefit of the students, their health and their ability to co-ordinate their body movements with efficiency and accuracy. It is the half-lotus position in which the ch'i (ki) is practiced. Some clubs advertise secret methods by which one may achieve inner strength (ch'i) in a relatively short period of time. However, in almost all cases these promises have proven to be fallacies. Several years of diligent practice under the instruction of a true master are unavoidable if one is seriously dedicated to the pursuit of such a strength. However, very few known masters are willing to teach students who have not proven themselves sincere and worthy of advanced and refined training. Because of the complexity and deep involvements of

Fig. 85

128

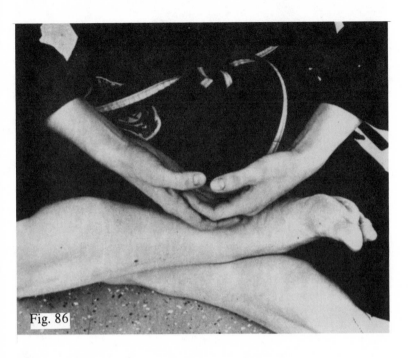

Fig. 86

meditation, only certain people are suitable to be trained. Within the group of Temple System schools, very, very few students are trained in the cultivation of the ch'i; and then they must be well advanced in their physical training before being accepted. The philosophical and the ethical opinions are against the introduction of this decisive knowledge to the general public. Our very competitive society would in no way benefit from a wide knowledge of the ch'i; rather, it would be the victim of much abuse, as man is always in search of miracles by which he can become greater than his fellowman. Having seen training methods and observed classes in which the ch'i is practiced, and having witnessed demonstrations of masters which supposedly possess "inner strength," might I suggest that one refuse mass training. The ch'i requires a very personal and individual effort and deserves serious respect on the part of its practitioner. No matter how well these training methods are explained in writing, without the guiding instruction of a teacher there will not be any true result. Those people who are self-taught unknowingly practice mistakes which become instilled in their muscle memory patterns. Since it takes such a long time before one develops inner strength, most students never continue preferring to concentrate on acquiring skill and competing in tournaments using sports Karate. Yet there are many people with the obsession to acquire all combative knowledge, regardless of source or system. These are the people which we commonly call "salesmen," for once they have lured the knowledge from each system they then begin to package it and place it on the market.

As far as conditioning is concerned, the Chinese did not actually use devices such as striking boards. (Fig. 87) They seemed to have been more interested in achieving inner force (invisible), which has proven even today to be far more effective than visible or outer strength. To be precise, the Moh system emphasizes both forms of strength in attaining the ultimate in skill and knowledge. A very important factor of any conditioning technique seems to be to what extent and for what purpose it should be practiced. Pounding a board or hammering with one's hand on table corners is, in my opinion, the most ignorant procedure followed in an attempt to acquire strength. No doubt, the desired effect, from the calluses formed, has been achieved, and the hand thus developed is fearful in appearance. Perhaps this is one of the reasons why the method of punching boards with great force is so popular. The Moh system, however, refuses this senseless pounding and inflicting of punishment upon the joints and bone structure. High-speed punches and an equally fast return of the delivered natural weapon should be the first step in training. If done in the air, the striking board cannot interfere with the speed of the punch nor delay the returning pull of the muscles. A new student, there-

Fig. 87

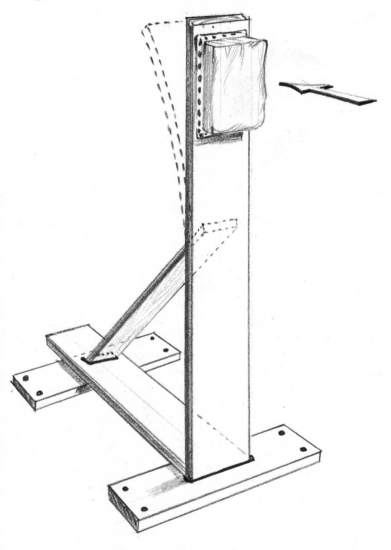

fore, should be interested in learning how to strike in empty space (air) and train himself at first in speed punching and kicking. Anyone interested in developing a solid bone structure without deforming the limbs should practice short blows against a hard surface executed at a distance of two to three inches from the object. These blows should be delivered fast (three to four per second) — in the beginning, loosely, without force, later increasing the power used. Through this form of vibration, the bone structure is compelled to build up resistance from the inside of the body rather than providing protection only on the outside, with a cushion of calluses. Developing one's natural weapons in this fashion requires more time and subsequently more patience, but the end result is far better, for one builds strong, hard hands and feet, which are lacking in callouses and joint damage, and reduces the pain of the delivering striking surface and secures forceful yet flexible muscles. For many young students, and especially for advanced Kung-fu men, it is their desire to remain with their art as long as possible. Thus, the wisdom of this ancient Chinese approach to conditioning can be appreciated, for it promises effectiveness even into the ripe and old ages.

The training of pushing and pulling force also deserves attention. A strong but pliable surface is preferable when training to strengthen the leg and arm muscles. Equipment such as the sand bag can be very helpful, as it allows for the execution of full striking force to form a strong wrist. It provides the best target when in motion (swinging), for one learns as well how to aim and develops a sense of timing. The outer casing of the bag offers resistance to attack very similar to that offered by the human body. If a bag is well supported from the ceiling and three to four feet off the ground many foot strikes can be practiced as well as hand-elbow and foot-knee combinations. (Fig. 88) One of the most ingenious inventions of the Chinese Shaolin Kung-fu schools was the rotating practice dummy. (Pg. 134) The purpose of this device was to provide the student with a prac-

Fig. 88

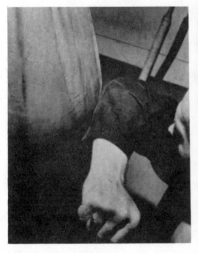

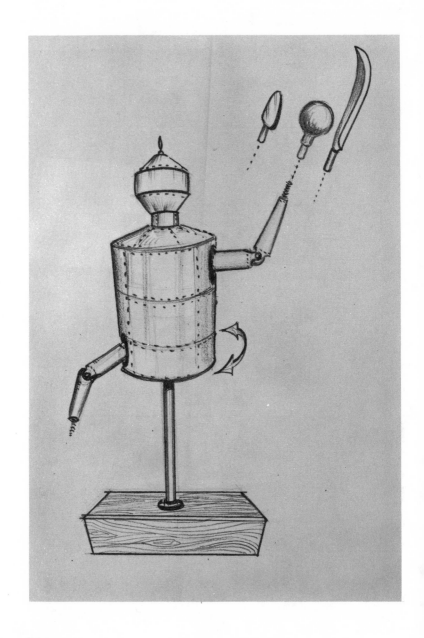

tice figure bearing a strong resemblance to the human body. The only flaw was that no foot strikes to the lower body areas could be trained, due to the type of mounting used. However, it was still of great value for training reflexes and muscle reactions. The adjustable arms were solidly mounted on the metal body and a strong block would swing the apparatus with great speed, causing the other arm to attack the training student and forcing him to turn to protect himself. Alternating between inside and outside blocking resulted in either an increase or a decrease in speed and force on the part of the rotating dummy. If the student failed to block an attack he would be struck. After such an experience, the effect was to encourage alertness and caution in the future. Without the knowledge of a blocking pattern and the system of interruption techniques, such a device loses most of its purpose and will be of little value. Only true knowledge can convert this device into a usable piece of training equipment. The Moh system stresses the use of pulling and turning blocks which evolve from the proper interrupting techniques in rotation blocking. As the art of blocking requires much skill in this style of Kung-fu, it is understandable that many years of practice are needed to master even the most basic forms involving these forceful circular thrusts and swinging body turns.

However, one can quite easily practice the inside and outside pulling block. (Fig. 89) Two students will oppose each other — one in a neutral position, the other in any ready or alert position. The offensive action should come from the neutral stance with a punch to the face. Using this level of attack, it is simple to study the block in question. As the punch is delivered, the blocking arm (Fig. 90) will lead the opponent's thrust away from the target — preferably to the outside of the body of the defending person — slide along his arm until the hand reaches the wrist of the opponent. Here it finds solid resistance because of the expanding sides of the palm. (Fig. 91) This is the best time to use a strong pulling technique. Only the thumb and the middle finger are used.

135

Fig. 89

Fig. 90   Fig. 91

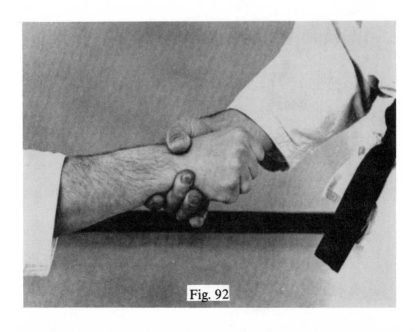

Fig. 92

Fig. 93

138

(Fig. 92) Successful application of this technique depends very much on speed, a strong grip and pulling power executed in the right direction. A student should immediately notice a poorly formed stance or an off-balance posture. Very often, it is the ability, in a combative situation, to recognize an opportunity to disturb the opponent's attack through a simple pull or push against the stance of the aggressor (Fig. 93), which decides the outcome. The padded

Fig. 93

stick is very popular for grabbing and pulling as well as blocking techniques. The versatility of motions, coming from all directions, which it allows for, leaves it unequaled by any other device and especially helpful for the training of foot blocks and circular stops. (Fig. 94) However, the more these training methods are understood, the more one will realize that only supervised instruction will satisfy and guarantee true skill.

Fig. 94

Fig. 94

For many Karate friends, the eighteen-inch practice ring is still an unknown training device. It aids in the development of the circular wrist and palm blocks and is good for the basic tensing exercises, which increase the pressing and lifting arm power. (below) Master Chojun Miyagi supposedly

has used his knowledge of the "ring" in devising some of the Goju-ryu tensing forms. A great many Karate men, however, will never learn the circular Kung-fu methods, for they prefer to continue within the training schedule of their own systems, using predominantly linear techniques. The Moh system combines a vast variety of circular foot and arm motions as well as the direct methods for which Karate has a feared reputation. To hit directly the opponent's foot with one's own foot, arm or fist is a brutal but effective method if one knows how to avoid receiving equal punishment in return. Operating in a circular fashion, in unison with advancing or retreating, changing from one stance to another, is a very involved part of the Moh System. The training ring only helps to strengthen and direct the movements so that they become both instinctive and accurate. However, learning how to block rapidly, forward and backward, using the wrist-over-wrist turning method can only be done under the guidance of a master. The interruption (or counter) movements are not usable for sports competition, and therefore need not be dealt with here.

Before ending this short explanation of the basic training methods, I shall introduce one section of the first set in the Moh system, which is called the "Awakening of the Dragon." Within these 219 movements there lies a vast wealth of knowledge. Beginning in a hard, straight line, this form evolves without being repetitious, into slow, soft motions stressing versatility of techniques and, most of all, the changing method of breathing. The seemingly worthless hand passages are in reality brutal dislocation holds which are to be applied against forceful strikes or kicks. Observing the following nineteen basic motions, one should imagine that formerly many years were spent repeating these movements over and over to attain the utmost in force and speed. Introduced as breathing and health exercises, they were done very slowly, and therefore should now be learned in a more moderate fashion. However, it is very helpful, both for the teacher and the student, at first to practice the forms slowly so that any mistake will be at once visible, especially loss of balance; this in particular is quite good to train for it is much harder to maintain balance while using less speed. At a later time, the student will learn to do the sections in these prearranged forms rapidly and with force. Actually, the solid floor of a gymnasium is a very unrealistic training ground. Grass or sand has a far different influence on jumps, steps and maneuvering ability. A smooth floor permits sliding and secure footing while in motion, whereas a rough surface, such as a gravel road, requires much more skill and concentration. If one is fortunate enough to train outdoors, on a lonesome beach or a river bank, this training will be as real as Nature itself. The fresh air and open spaces will rejuvenate the mind and body, encouraging far better results and a more thorough enjoyment of the Temple System.

BLOCKING

Fig. 95

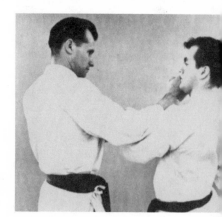

Introduction

Upon introduction to these blocking techniques, one may notice the extreme similarity between them and those of other styles. Perhaps it is because this is one portion of the combative arts upon which there seems to be general agreement. For instance, to block an attack, in the form of a punch or a kick, always requires more direct contact, especially if the oncoming attack possesses great force. Aiming at a nerve center would be a form of position blocking, the purpose of which is to slow down the actions of the opponent. Another approach is the simple deflection of the attack. Here, rather than stopping the movement of the assailant, one diverts his attack to a different direction in order to take better advantage of his force and body motion. The limbs themselves cannot be damaged as neatly or effectively, neither do they offer vulnerable nerve centers as compared to some vital points located on the body, which show an immediate effect after being attacked. Many magazines, in their illustrations of these vital areas, include the wrist joint. In reality, there is not much damage one could do to the wrist joint, and the foolish attempt to concentrate on this target will prove a rather dangerous practice. (Fig. 95)

The Basic Arm Blocks

The inside block, which can be executed with a knife hand, a forearm or a closed fist, is a blocking line preferable for use in the middle area of the body. Its basic movement is directed from the inside defense area to the inside of the opponent's attacking limb. (Fig. 96) The outside block (to the middle area) would thus come from the outside of one's body to the outside of the opponent's attacking limb. (Fig. 97) Of course, if stepping and body movements are combined, an inside block can be applied to the outside of the attacking arm (foot); and (Fig. 98) an outside block can be delivered to the inside of the attacking arm. This proves very effective against a swinging punch to the head. (Fig. 99) One of the universal methods of stopping a high attack to the head is the use of the high forearm block. (Fig. 100) The elbow joint is bent at an approximate angle of 90° and the fist is turned to the outside. (Fig. 101) After blocking

Fig. 96

Fig. 97

Fig. 98

Fig. 99

Fig. 100

Fig. 101

Fig. 102

Fig. 103

the opponent's attack, a counterattack, if executed properly, can be very effective. (Fig. 102) The block in Figure 102 can be easily converted into a high hooking block by simply opening the fists and turning the palms to the outside while in motion. (Fig. 103)

Blocking downward, to provide protection against foot strikes, is most effective when maintaining a deep stance. A poor stance endangers one's ability to completely protect the lower body area and tempts the defending person into leaning forward. (Fig. 104) As the central balance is gradually broken, the head comes within reach of the assailant's fists. A strike to the head in such a position (Fig. 105) could be

150

Fig. 104

Fig. 105

151

fatal. The blocking technique begins with the arm positioned on the opposite shoulder (here the left fist is brought on the right shoulder), the bottom of the fist touching. As the left arm is brought down, withdraw the right arm into a ready striking position. (Fig. 106) Following the same procedure,

Fig. 106

but turning one's front bow stance to the side (here a left bow turning right) and opening the blocking hand, one may redirect the foot strike to the back of one's stance. (Fig. 107)

Fig. 107

Many of the special arm and hand blocking methods are not mentioned, as they are part of the movements introduced in the "weeping willow." These motions involve the entire body, using a method not known to most Karate students and therefore are not usable material for training the basics of the Moh system. The open hand wrist block ending in an elbow strike (Fig. 108), the cross blocking methods (Fig. 109), and the hooking blocks and throws are very specialized and detailed. Along with many other advanced blocking methods, they are left for explanation in a more advanced text.

Fig. 108

Fig. 109

The Basic Foot Blocks

If certain styles have acquired a reputation for their re-markable skill — in the case of the Korean styles it would be for their brilliant kicking feats, and in the Japanese styles for their classic and firm motions — the Moh system would then be known for its short and powerful as well as long and graceful movements, specializing in foot maneuvers and body-shifting techniques, at one moment solid and firm, then altogether different, exhibiting short, catlike dances with very deep, narrow stances, changing rapidly from the explosive to the softly flowing, going from one technique to the next.

During the explanation, we have already shown some of the important foot blocks, but in order that they may be learned accurately I shall discuss them again. These blocks may be classified according to the three main sections of the body (below).

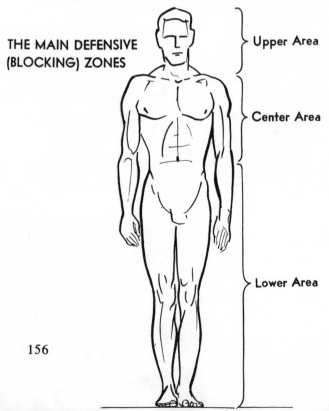

THE MAIN DEFENSIVE (BLOCKING) ZONES

Upper Area

Center Area

Lower Area

To the centre of the body one may deliver the inside foot block. Using the sole of the foot (Fig. 110), the shin bone or the side of the foot (knife edge), this block comes from the inside of one's own position to the inside of the opponent's limb. Depending on the opponent's movements and one's own position during an attack, the inside foot block can also be applied against the outside of the attacking foot. (Fig. 111) However, one must know how to change one's

Fig. 110

Fig. 111

own position swiftly in order to stop the kick and perhaps throw the assailant. (Fig. 112) The outside foot block (motion to the center, executed to the outside of the opponent's attacking limb) operates in much the same fashion as the inside foot block, except that it is done in the opposite direction. For the effective application of an outside foot block one requires good stepping skill and maneuverability. (Fig. 113)

A high punch may be stopped by the foot, but this requires great flexibility and control. In an extreme case, where the opponent is much taller than the defending person, one should use the arms for secure and accurate blocking. A direct high kick under the arm is possible only if one is very well trained. In this kick (Fig. 114), the striking arm of the opponent is blocked by the defender's opposite foot, using the ball of the foot as a striking surface. Much more secure and equally as effective is the high cross kick, using the sole of the foot against the same attack. (Fig. 115)

Fig. 112

Fig.

Fig. 114

Fig. 115

All low blocking foot strikes are directed against the leg movements of the opponent only. An extremely effective method of stopping an attack to the groin is the use of the sole of the foot in blocking the opponent's leg. (Fig. 116)

Fig. 116

It is of great importance to execute this block fairly high in order to avoid being hurt by an attempted high kick, wherein the opponent would lift his kick over one's blocking kick and then attack. (Fig. 117) However, the distance and position from which all of these blocks are executed must be such that the defending person is able quickly to recognize any intended maneuver of assault. Only experience will assure the good choice of a position for the effective application of blocks and counter techniques. A large variety of foot-blocking strikes are meant to maim the ankle, knee, calf or instep, and should therefore be practiced by a good-minded person. (Fig. 118) Throughout this book, I have avoided

Fig. 117

Fig. 118

exploiting cruelty, and thus have only mentioned certain techniques (attack to the eyes, throat, groin). Once aware of their existence, the student is made to realize the danger he may face, and is thus, indirectly, encouraged to learn his blocks and counter techniques, evasions and throws ·well enough so that he need not fear such assaults.

In this basic introduction of the Moh system, I have introduced its philosophy, its aim and some of its basic techniques. The knowledge surrounding the Moh system is so vast that it would require many volumes before everything were introduced. To explain the breathing methods for the training of the ch'i, the movements of the "weeping willow," the rotation lifting blocks, the vertical cutting blocks and the "planets' circles" demands explicit illustrations and detailed coverage in each and every field of these groups of movements. Many of these motions have never been shown before and therefore are still considered to be secrets of the Moh system. The relationship between this system and the modern Kung-fu systems is barely visible. However, the value of many of these combative movements is unsurpassed, and thus should be preserved so that they may remain pure and untainted.

KICKING

Fig. 119

Fig. 12

Front Kick

The most helpful position to assume while learning the front kick is the front bow stance. (Fig. 119) The right foot is brought to the centre and raised so that the knee shows a 90° angle if observed from the side. (Fig. 120) Now the foot is thrown forward, the toes are bent up and back (Fig. 121) and the instep arched and fully extended. The entire body may never lean away from the target (here the centre of the opponent's body), rather it should point slightly in the striking direction. (Fig. 122) The supporting leg is kept bent at the knee and the heel should not be raised. When using extreme force while practising without a target, the heel will be somewhat raised. This, however, is not a serious mistake. Observing the correct striking distance should enable the student to show a slightly bent knee at the moment

Fig. 121

Fig. 122

of contact. (Fig. 123) The immediate withdrawal of the kicking leg, while still maintaining good balance, back to the beginning position (Fig. 124) is extremely important. The front kick may also be executed high or low. (Fig. 125)

Fig. 123

Fig. 124

Fig. 125

167

Roundhouse Kick

Assume a left forward stance. (Fig. 126) The heel of the striking foot is only inches above the knee; in fact, the knee and heel are almost in a horizontal position. (Fig. 127) This foot maneuver should be executed from an offset angle, the toes being bent well back as they make contact. (Fig. 128) In all punching and striking techniques one has to concentrate on withdrawing the attack as quickly as it was executed. Most foot strikes, especially, should be trained in this fashion. A foot which is not withdrawn immediately after the execution of a kick will disturb one's balance and not permit a successful defense if facing more than one opponent at a time. Leaving an arm or a leg close to the target for too long gives the opponent the opportunity of breaking the joints. (Fig. 129) Aside from this, one is not able to repeat the techniques fast enough, and this allows the opponent time to counter one's own attack. This kick may also be done high (Fig. 130) and low (Fig. 131).

Fig. 126

Fig. 127

Fig. 128

Fig. 129

Fig. 130

Fig. 131

Side Kick

While learning the side kick, one of the best positions to assume is the open crane stance, in which the supporting leg is bent. (Fig. 132) Using a side kick from this position provides a very effective method of countering. (Fig. 133)

Fig. 132

Fig. 133

The leg, however, must be withdrawn immediately after striking. The knife edge of the foot is used, with the emphasis being on the end (heel) of the foot, for better protection and more impact force. (Fig. 134) Note the pictures showing a high side kick (Fig. 135) and a low side kick. (Fig. 136)

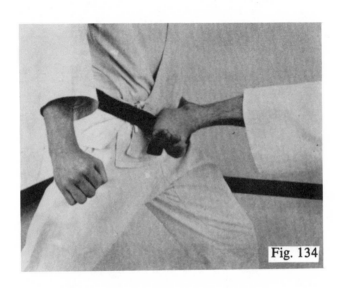

Fig. 134

Fig. 135

Fig. 136

Back Kick

Assume a left forward stance. (Fig. 137) This kick is executed after a short spinning turn and a foregoing block. (Fig. 138) Whether delivered low (Fig. 139), to the centre (Fig. 140) or high (Fig. 141), the heel is always pointing strongly towards the target.

Fig. 137

Fig. 138

Fig. 139

Fig. 140

Fig. 141

A FEW WORDS ON BREAKING

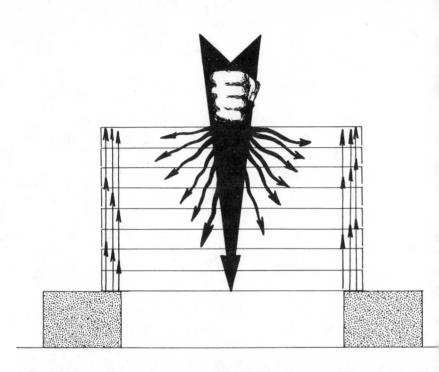

The "superhuman force" and Karate are constantly publicized as one and the same thing. Television and radio stations, knowing little of the art, use sensationalism in their promotion of it. However, when they speak of superhuman or supernatural force, they are attempting to convey the idea that the common man cannot possess this power. This, of course, is not true. Any person is able to train his body to do almost anything, providing he is willing to work hard and long. Whether or not one must be capable of breaking several bricks in order to be called an "expert" is beside the point. Breaking is a simple method of exhibiting great explosive force. To be quite frank, breaking is done by most advanced students and has proven to be an example of totally human force. Labeling it the result of superhuman strength is unrealistic, dishonest and hyperbolic. Having in the past met many students and instructors, I observed that a great percentage do not own the true force and that their applied force on boards and stones differs very much from what I have been taught. Many of these people have practiced according to the explanations given in books, and almost all of them possessed the same reasoning, as far as their methods of applying power, most of which was nothing but brutal physical force. Only a very few of these people bothered to breathe or position their bodies correctly for the effective support of their blows. In the Orient one can observe performers who are willing to break bricks and plates for a small sum of money. Doing this without having any scientific knowledge whatsoever has caused crippling in their arms and hands. Other side effects become apparent only when one has reached an advanced age. This indulgence in primitive glory finds its nemesis in the form of cancer and other permanent bone damage.

But, as in all things, it is the intelligent approach, plus knowledge, which secures workable results. If breaking exhibitions are really a demonstration of skill and power then they should be done by a master who has understood the value of the philosophy of Karate and refuses the unnecessary sensational glorification which breaking attracts. Though this is not meant as an encouragement for the student to train himself for breaking, I will, however, now introduce the Chinese approach to the delivery of explosive power by mentioning certain fundamental points:

(1) right preparation
(2) right distance
(3) right position
(4) right striking angle
(5) right breathing
(6) right ch'i force
(7) right timing
(8) right aim
(9) right impact force
(10) right ending force

SELF-DEFENSE

I. Introduction

I.

The Shaolin System of Kung-fu is renowned for possessing the ultimate in self-defense knowledge. Contrary to public opinion, a vast knowledge of the methods of self-defense does not guarantee the best results when protecting oneself. Knowledge in the martial arts must be combined with skill; also, only when theory is put into practice will it secure a safe defense.

A course in self-defense is as unrealistic as a six-week course in surgery, for it is ridiculous to expect that knowledge can be immediately put into safe practice. Knife attacks are extremely dangerous, as most criminals are well versed in the use of this weapon. Many defenses shown against a weapon such as a knife are preposterous. It is interesting to note that only a very few books have specifically indicated that the author had true skill and knowledge.

II. Subsequent books such as
   'Anti-Rape' cover this subject
   in far greater detail.

THE GRADING SYSTEM

The ancient Chinese had their very own standard of proficiency. The self-defense societies could recognize one another only by means of a color code. It is believed that this code evolved from military groups which used certain traditional color banners to show their loyalty to their king. Through the introduction of Judo, some of these colors have been introduced, using a newly invented color system in which the rank is indicated by the color worn. The sash was replaced by a belt, and thus the legendary black belt came into being.

In the Moh system the four ranks awarded apply to the span of life and, in comparison with Nature, describe the stages of learning and the development towards perfection.

Green — represents Spring
Blue — represents Summer
Red   — represents Fall
White — represents Winter

The many different systems have, through participation in sports competitions and for the purpose of universal understanding, accepted the idea of accrediting high skill with the black belt, or "dan," degree. Starting with the first dan and continuing as far as the eleventh dan, they represent true skill only until the fifth dan is achieved. All ranks after the fifth dan are honorary awards and used primarily for prestige reasons. As the number eight is mathematically of higher value than the number seven, the question of due respect seems to be resolved.

Within the International Temple Kung-fu Association¹, the use of foreign terminology has been abolished, as these words have nothing in common with our tradition and only tend to credit the Orient with a supremacy in the arts. The wealth of knowledge available on our continent, if exchanged amongst the existing Karate and Kung-fu styles, is of such a gigantic nature that it would at once place our countries one hundred years ahead of all the Oriental nations.

Color	*Grade*
white belt	8th
yellow belt	7th
orange belt	6th
green belt	5th
blue belt	4th
Brown Level One	3rd
Brown Level Two	2nd
Brown Level Three	1st
black belt	1st degree
	2nd degree
	3rd degree
	4th degree

	Kung-fu Master
red belt	5th degree
	6th degree
	7th degree
	8th degree
	9th degree
	10th degree
	11th degree

EPILOGUE

Many generations ago, Kung-fu — today better known as Karate — was brought to the North American continent by Chinese immigrants. It was not actually introduced to the people of the Western world for a long time after this, as the Chinese had a tendency to cling to their own family system and thus were unwilling to teach Kung-fu to foreigners. But old customs soon give way to modern thinking, for simple logic tells one that the most perfect skill cannot compare with the modern weapons of the space age. After the introduction of sports Karate by the Japanese, the Chinese also succumbed to modern thinking. It is the contribution of the Chinese of their deep and refined knowledge which has rejuvenated the art and rebuilt its ethical and philosophical foundations. Civilization has established law and order, and the Western world of today is well governed and protected. Kung-fu however, has not taken its place among the ancients, for it still is of value to the world. Modern police forces now train their staff in Kung-fu so that they can maintain peace without fear of being themselves injured or killed. Chinese Kung-fu especially, offers a vast variety of self-defense techniques, from kicking and punching to the throwing of an opponent. However, possessing force equal to that of one's opponent does not necessarily mean that one is capable of receiving equal punishment. Therefore, a smaller and much weaker person is trained to avoid being hit by making use of the aggressor's strength to benefit his own counter movements.

The Oriental fighting arts have found many friends and practitioners on this continent. Anyone seriously involved in

188

these arts has come to appreciate the many benefits which are connected with them. Karate, especially, has enjoyed a success unparalleled by all other combative arts. Its lively spirit and rapid movements fascinate any viewer who has a heart for contact sports and a love for skillful exhibitions. The continued interest in this particular combative art has led to the most outstanding promotion any sport has ever received. At first, it was the term Karate, then Kempo, now finally Kung-fu which labels the superforce of the trained hand. Soon the rush was on. Many clever operators, having observed the rising trend in public interest, quickly changed the image of Karate so that it became a deadly cult promoting the "tough" way of life. Books were sold under the guise of revealing in their pages "never before told secrets" of the Orient, offering in actuality tricks which, once learned, were enough to startle the layman, but in truth were completely useless and foreign to the true training methods. Next, the public was made to think that the only true Karate man was the Oriental protege of a great master. Certain people have even gone so far as to change their diet, to live as close to the ground as possible — as one does in the Karate countries — and to change their religion. Since distance separates them from the true tradition and culture of these countries, they try to create, through imitation, the same atmosphere in their own country. In many cases, such persons possess a very sparse knowledge of their own country's valuable history and have failed to integrate into creative fields, of which our Western culture provides so many. Often it is this type of individual who sells the art by offering package deals and sending out sales representatives to recruit new "customers." Apparently, for only a small sum of money, one may practice this ancient art and share in the honor and spirit which was once attained by the highly respected bushido men, the Samurai.

In reality, there is no "salesman-to-customer" approach in a reputable establishment. At one time, it was fitting that the student helped his master in the house or on the field to show his appreciation for having been given the privilege of being instructed by him. The modern world has simplified this connection, and the close relationship between student and master has been lost. The over-evaluation of money and the temptation which success offers encourage the student to begin on his own before he is fully equipped to do so, like a bird trying to fly before his wings have been formed. These teenage "masters" surround themselves with friends to establish security, then pursue the "tough line" in an attempt to conceal their own lack of thorough knowledge and refined skill. The saddest example of loyalty and respect is shown when a student opposes his former master by opening his own school just across the street from him. At one time an unthinkable act, this has now become quite a common occurrence. Ethics seems to be defeated by the inhuman desire to achieve success at all costs, this feeling being encouraged, I might add, by our modern school of thought. In books and pamphlets we can read the "do's and don'ts" of success in life — how to get a better-paid job with less effort and how to outdo one's fellowman in any profession. The "advertised honor" is enough to satisfy the conscience of the newly enrolled student, who has often committed himself for a lengthy period of time and for a fair sum of money. After all, honor and enlightenment are not advertised as much in other sports as in Karate, which offers one the true "warrior's honor"; for, as one Karate promoter explains, "The student now learns how to die." The price — one membership. No special education is necessary on the part of the student in order to make such a skill available to him, as Nature itself takes care of all life in its very own way.

The great religions are far better equipped to prepare us for this unavoidable moment. Many of our countrymen have died in honor defending the principles of our heritage. Even now they are giving their lives, committing themselves to a far greater code of humanity than the simple motto which states, "Karate is a way of learning how to die." This motto, breathes of neither wisdom nor common sense. Kung-fu, most definitely, finds no fullfilment in such paper-thin words. The Moh system, **or Temple System,** has been derived from a far different source of philosophy altogether. It is not brutal force nor blind courage which will conquer fear, but the experienced knowledge of the results of pain, the continuing refusal of force through the most skillful mastering of one's mind and body and, finally, the attainment of such a universal strength as to desire nothing else but the enlightenment of all men in order that peace may be brought to each and every one of us.

Having seen fear and destruction,
and having felt pain and sorrow,
I was well prepared by my master.
If there is evil, hate and distrust,
I then shall face danger with courage,
refusing all weapons
with Kung-fu— the law of the fist.
The skill of the weaponless hand
will turn then upon those
who dared to dishonor or harm
the quiet reign of blessingful peace.

FAMOUS
CHINESE KUNG-FU SYSTEMS

Shao-lin-ssu
Ch'uan-shu
Pa-kua
Chiao-ti
Hua-chuan
Shou-pu
Hung
Ts'ai
Fut
Wing Chuan Pai
Li
Liu
Hung Fut Pai
Ponghai-noon
Wu Tang Shan
Choy Li Fut Pai
Tong Long Pai
Bak Hok Pai
Tai Chi Chuan
Kang Fa
Jou Fa
MOH (TEMPLE) SYSTEM

Tiger
Bear
Monkey
Fowl
Leopard
Dragon
Crane

These movements are part of almost all styles.

All forms of present day Karate (Judo, Aikido, Jiu-jitsu) also have been derived from these Chinese systems.

APPLICATION OF THE MOH (TEMPLE) SYSTEM

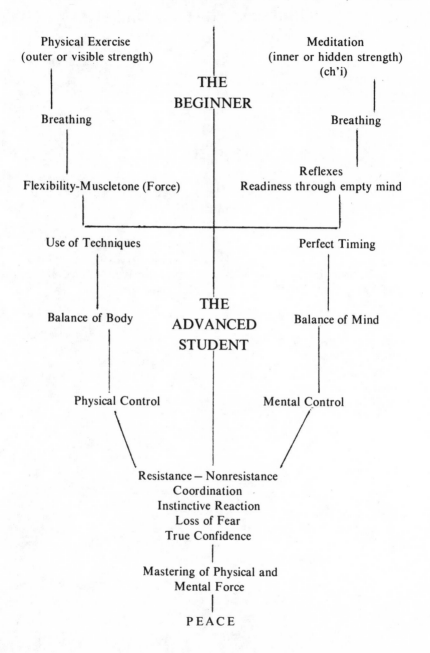

Physical Exercise
(outer or visible strength)

Meditation
(inner or hidden strength)
(ch'i)

**THE
BEGINNER**

Breathing

Breathing

Flexibility-Muscletone (Force)

Reflexes
Readiness through empty mind

Use of Techniques

Perfect Timing

Balance of Body

**THE
ADVANCED
STUDENT**

Balance of Mind

Physical Control

Mental Control

Resistance — Nonresistance
Coordination
Instinctive Reaction
Loss of Fear
True Confidence

Mastering of Physical and
Mental Force

PEACE

A FEW OF THE
EIGHTEEN

TEMPLE MOVEMENTS

You may not always succeed
but you know that you will
never cease trying.

The temple needs no words,
no explanation.
It stand for firmness, kindness
and non betrayal -
virtues which today are seldom
encountered.

The birds shall remind you
of the many commandments
all of mankind shares:
that you have a share
in the making
of a better person
by trying to become tolerant
towards differences.

Thus the sign of the temple,
wherever you find it,
will remind you
that someone else
is trying as well.

OTHER BOOKS BY THE AUTHOR:

The Adventure Series:
Volume I - The White Priest
Volume II - Takuan the Manchurian
Volume III - The Tigers of Sinkiang
Volume IV - The Lost Jade
Volume V - The Living Arrow
Volume VI - The Soul of Emptiness
Volume VII - The Borders of Heaven
Volume VIII - Reincarnation of the Tiger

Technical Work:
Anti-Rape & Total Self-Defense